# Made for You

# Made for You

## HOMEMADE GIFTS TO GIVE

NEW
HOLLAND

# JENNY OCCLESHAW

First published in 2013 by
New Holland Publishers
London • Sydney • Cape Town • Auckland
www.newhollandpublishers.com • www.newholland.com.au

The Chandlery Unit 114 50 Westminster Bridge Road London SE1 7QY
1/66 Gibbes Street Chatswood NSW 2067 Australia
Wembley Square First Floor Solan Road Gardens Cape Town 8001 South Africa
218 Lake Road Northcote Auckland New Zealand

A catalogue record of this book is available at the British Library and at the National Library of Australia

ISBN: 9781742574158

10 9 8 7 6 5 4 3 2 1

Publisher: Lliane Clarke
Designer: Tracy Loughlin
Editor: Simona Hill
Photographer: Natalie Hunfalvay
Illustrator: Steve Dew
Production director: Olga Dementiev
Printer: Toppan Leefung Printing Limited

Follow New Holland Publishers on
Facebook: www.facebook.com/NewHollandPublishers

# Contents

# Introduction

This is a book for all of us who love to make beautiful items and bestow them upon an appreciative audience. Handmade gifts are often cherished by those who understand the time and effort that has been put into making them. And for those of us who love to sew, knit and crochet, there is the delicious anticipation of planning a project and the tactile experience of choosing yarns or cloth and selecting the perfect trims.

   This collection of projects is not just beautiful to look at but practical too. This was an important factor for me, since many of these projects take time, energy and expense to make. Perhaps you have a new addition to the family and are keen to flex your creative muscle? There are plenty of knitted garments here that are small in scale, use minimal yarn and are quick to make. A sweet little baby bloomer vest and knickers set is perfect for a newborn. Knitted in silky soft yarn that's kind to baby's skin, this is a project that will be a delight to make. For a favourite friend there are beautiful knitted, felted, needle-felted and embroidered brooches to make. These use plenty of different skills, and being small can be made in no time at all. They also give you chance to sample lots of different craft skills without too much outlay. For the men in your life there are scarves and socks to knit, all in beautiful yarns that will wear well and last a lifetime. There are plenty of items here too that you might like to make just for the fun of it – a pin cushion perhaps or a snuggly pair of gloves. Who knows, you may find it impossible to give away your creations after you've lavished time and attention on them.

   Whatever you choose, no item is too large that it cannot be made quickly and consequently none will be too costly to make. Whatever you make, have fun!

# Essential Techniques

None of the projects featured in this book are difficult to master. You'll need to be able to knit and some crochet skills would be useful. The most complicated techniques are described here.

## Grafting Knitting

This is an excellent way of invisibly joining two pieces of knitting. The edges are not cast off and the knitting can be joined either while it is still on the needles or after it has been taken off.

1 With the stitches to be grafted on parallel, double-pointed needles, make sure that the working yarn is coming from the back needle.

2 Take the wool needle through the first stitch on the front needle as if to purl and leave the stitch on the needle. Now, go through the first

stitch on the back needle as if to knit and leave this stitch on the needle.

3 Keep the working yarn below the needles, work two stitches on the front needle, followed by two stitches on the back needle, across the row, as follows:

On the front needle, go through the first stitch as if to knit and drop it off the needle. Go through the second stitch as if to purl and leave it on the needle. Tighten the yarn.

On the back needle, go through the first stitch as if to purl and drop it off the needle. Go through the second stitch as if to knit and leave it on the needle. Tighten the yarn.

When there is only 1 st on each needle, go through the front stitch as if to knit and drop it off the needle. Go through the back stitch as if to purl and drop it off the needle. Pull the tail to the inside and weave in.

## Making a Crocheted Slip Ring

A slip ring does not have any stitches.

Grasp the yarn in your left hand, between your thumb and index finger, and allow the yarn to flow freely over your index finger. Support the yarn with your middle finger. Leave a tail of yarn trailing below your thumb.

Grasp your hook in your right hand, between your thumb, index finger and middle finger. Use the same type of tension that you would use to hold a pen; your fingers should be relaxed enough to move freely, but they should grip tightly enough to maintain precise control over the hook. To start, keep the hook facing upward.

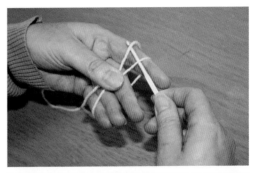

**1** Insert the crochet hook between your index finger and the yarn. You can insert it either from left to right or from right to left. The photo shows the hook being inserted from right to left.

**2** Use the crochet hook to twist the yarn so that a loose loop is on the hook.

You should still be holding the tail of yarn between your index finger and thumb. Your middle finger, fourth finger and pinkie can be used to manipulate the other end of the yarn as it unwinds from the ball.

**3** Use your crochet hook to hook the yarn and draw it through the loop. Be sure to hook the end that is still attached to the ball, not the tail of the yarn that is between your thumb and forefinger.

**4** You should now have a loose slip knot on your crochet hook. It will need tightening. Leave it on the crochet hook and tug gently on both ends of yarn to tighten it up. Don't over-tighten it; the crochet hook should be able to move easily inside this loop so that you can form your starting chain in the next step. You can now crochet into the slip ring to begin your flower and then pull on the end to tighten it.

## Needle Felting

Needle felting is a quick and easy way to add embellishment to plain felted knitting. The technique fuses a layer of fiber (wool roving, wool yarn, or another piece of felt) onto a base layer of fabric. To begin needle felting you will need to gather a few supplies, all of which should be available at your local craft store:

A needle felting brush or piece of foam (I prefer the brush), which allows the needles to go through the fiber and beyond without damaging the needles or the surface below

A needle-felting tool, either a single needle or a specific tool which has four needles inside a plastic sleeve can be used

Wool roving in various colours, or wool yarn or cut out pieces of felt

A felted swatch to practise on or your piece of felted knitting.

**1** Decide how you would like the finished needle-felting embellishment to look. You can make it as simple as adding stripes, dots, shapes or any other design. Working in small sections, tear or cut a piece of roving and arrange it in place on the ground fabric. Start with less roving than you think you need – you can always add more. If you're using yarn as your needle-felting material, start with one strand. For a felted shape, simply put it in place where you'd like it to be and you're ready to begin needle felting.

**2** Put your base fabric on the needle-felting brush or foam, then position the fibre on top. If you have a needle-felting tool, unlock the sleeve. If you have a single needle, it's ready to go. Though it's pretty obvious, it's worth mentioning that both kinds of needle-felting needles are extremely sharp and can do a lot of damage to you and/or your tabletop if not used properly. That's why you should always work with a brush or piece of foam under your work. You could take the added measure of covering the table to protect it. To protect your fingers, keep them out of the way of the needles at all times, and always make sure you lock your needle-felting tool if you're going to store it or leave it unattended. The best approach for needle felting is to jab with a straight up and down motion using the needle. Try to go in as straight as possible; this makes it less likely you'll break the needle. The needle pushes the fibres into the ground fabric. The more you jab with the needle the more secure the fibres will be.

**3** Start at one end of your line or shape and work your way around by jabbing with the needle. If needle felting a large shape, start by needle felting around the outside and work your way in. The more you puncture the fibres with the needle-felting tool, the more fused the base fabric and your design will become. If you were to pull your fabric up off the brush or foam piece, you'd be able to see the fibres of the roving or yarn coming through the back of the felted fabric. Once you have a consistent amount of fibre peeking through the back your needle felting is complete. Really it's a matter of personal preference; keep going until you think it's time to stop.

**4** Trim any fibre that runs over the edge of your piece, and go back over those edges to make sure they're firmly fused to the background fabric. You may have other errant strands that didn't quite felt as well as the others that you can either go back over or trim away from the work as well. The final phase is all about making the work look crisp and, well, finished.

## KNITTING AND FELTING YARN

Some pure wool yarns can be felted in a washing machine. Other yarns are specifically manufactured to be knitted and then felted. The friction and heat of the drum action causes the fibres to shrink and mat together.

**1** Using 5 mm (¼ in) knitting needles and felting yarn, cast on 50 sts using 5 mm knitting needles. The tension does not matter. Work 2 rows garter st. Continue in stocking st until the yarn has been used. Cast off.

**2** If you have a front-loading washing machine put the knitted piece in a zipped cushion cover. Add a towel and six tennis balls. I wash knitted felting yarn using this cycle twice to get 40 per cent shrinkage. For a top-loading washing machine use a short, hot cycle with no spin followed by quickly immersing the piece in cold water to cause the felting.

**3** Once the felted piece is washed gently pull it into shape and then leave it to dry over a clothes airer or hang on a hanger in the bathroom. When dry, press flat with a warm iron under a damp cloth.

**4** To finish the edges of the felted piece, whip stitch around the edge by hand using a matching thread.

## KNITTING ABBREVIATIONS

**Cm**: Centimetres

**Garter Stitch**: Knit every row.

**Inc**: Increase by knitting into front and back of next stitch

**K**: Knit

**M1**: Make 1 – pick up the loop that lies between the two needles and knit into the back of it, place on right-hand needle.

**Moss Stitch**:

Rows 1 and 4: K1, * p1, k1; rep from * to end of row.

Rows 2 and 3: P1,* k1, p1; rep from * to end of row.

Repeat Rows 1–4 to create the pattern.

**P**: Purl

**Patt**: Pattern

**PSSO**: Pass slipped stitch over

**Rem**: Remaining

**Rep**: Repeat

**RS**: Right side

**Sl**: Slip

**St(s)**: Stitch(es)

**St st**: Stocking stitch: Knit one row, purl one row

**Tbl**: Through back of loops

**Tog**: Together

**WS**: Wrong side

**Yfwd**: Yarn forward – bring yarn to front of work, under right hand needle.

**Yon**: The same as yarn around needle, this creates a stitch. So bring yarn right round the needle and take to the back of the work to create an extra stitch, which will be knitted on the next row.

**Yo**: Same as above.

## CROCHET ABBREVIATIONS

**Ch**: Chain

**Dc**: Double crochet

**Dbl tr**: Double treble

**Htr**: Half treble

**Sp**: space

**Ss**: Slip stitch

**Tr**: Treble

**Tt Tt**: Triple treble

## YARN CONVERSIONS

| UK/Australia | US |
|---|---|
| 1 ply | lace weight |
| 2 ply | baby |
| 3 ply | fingering |
| 4 ply | sport weight |
| 8 ply, double knit (DK) | worsted weight |
| 10 ply, Aran | fisherman or medium |
| 12 ply, chunky | bulky |

If the needle size suggested is 4 mm and your tension is too tight on this size you should try 4.5 mm. If your tension is too loose try 3.75 mm. i.e one size up or down.

## Knitting Needle Size Conversions

| Metric (mm) | UK | US |
|---|---|---|
| 1 mm | | |
| 2 mm | 14 | 0 |
| 2.25 mm | 13 | 1 |
| 2.75 mm | 12 | 2 |
| 3 mm | 11 | 2/3 |
| 3.25 mm | 10 | 3 |
| 3.75 mm | 9 | 5 |
| 4 mm | 8 | 6 |
| 4.5 mm | 7 | 7 |
| 5 mm | 6 | 8 |
| 5.5 mm | 5 | 9 |
| 6 mm | 4 | 10 |
| 6.5 mm | 3 | 10½ |
| 7 mm | 2 | 10½ |
| 7.5 mm | 1 | 11 |

## Crochet Hook Conversions

| Metric (mm) | UK | US (Closest equivalent) |
|---|---|---|
| 0.4 | - | - |
| 0.6 | - | 6 Steel |
| 0.75 | 5 | 14 Steel |
| 1 | 4 | 12 |
| 1.25 | 3 | - |
| 1.5 | 2½ | 8 |
| 1.75 | 2 | 6 |
| 2 | 14 standard | 0 standard |
| 2.5 | 12 | 1½ |
| 3 | 11 | 2½ |
| 3.25 | 10 | D/3 |
| 3.5 | 9 | E/4 |
| 4 | 8 | F/5 |
| 4.5 | 7 | G/6 |
| 5 | 6 | H/8 |
| 5.5 | 5 | I/9 |
| 6 | 4 | J/10 |
| 7 | 2 | K1/4 |
| 8 | 0 | L/11 |
| 9 | 00 | M/13 |
| 10 | 000 | N/15 |

# Stitch Directory

## Back Stitch

The back stitch can be used to produce a relatively strong seam, resembling machine stitching. Take a stitch back about 2 mm ($^1/_{16}$ in) long, depending on the fabric, and then pull the needle through the fabric. For a stronger seam, take a small back stitch from time to time.

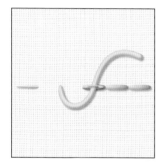

## Ladder Stitch

A ladder stitch can be used to join two hemmed edges together invisibly. Bring the needle through the fold of the hem to the right side of the fabric. Take a stitch directly opposite into the right side of the fold of the second hem. Run the needle a short distance up the inside of the fold and bring the needle out to the right side. Take a stitch into the original fold directly opposite and run it a short distance up the inside of the fold. Continue as set.

## Stem Stitch

Bring the thread out at A and hold it down with the thumb. Insert the needle at B and bring it out at C, midway between A and B.

Pull the thread through to see the first stitch. Hold the working thread down with the thumb and insert the needle at D, bringing it out at B.

Insert the needle at E and bring it out at D. Continue in this way, making each stitch exactly the same length.

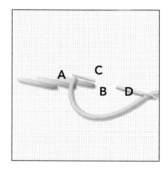

## Blind-hemming Stitch

Take a stitch in the hem edge. Take a small stitch in the garment just below the first stitch, at the same time putting the needle in the hem edge at least 6 mm ($^1/_4$ in) ahead; pull the needle through the fabric. Continue along the length.

## Blanket Stitch

Work this stitch along straight or curved lines on the fabric surface.

Bring the needle up from the lower left edge and insert the needle through the fabric at the top of the location of the first stitch.

Bring the tip of the needle through the fabric a short distance below the entry point, making a vertical stitch. If working along a marked line, the needle tip is brought through the fabric to the right side. If it is worked along an edge, the needle tip extends beyond the edge of the fabric.

Pull the needle through to make an I-shaped half loop with the embroidery thread. Continue working the stitch, spacing each a short distance apart at regular intervals.

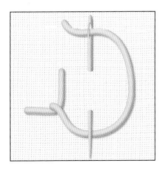

## Whip Stitch

The whip stitch is used to hold two folded edges together in a tight narrow seam. Place the two edges together. Take the stitches from back to front, close to the fold and close together.

## Satin Stitch

Basic satin stitch is an easy filling stitch that can be used to fill small areas.

Bring the needle up through the fabric at the starting point (A).

Insert the needle on the opposite side of the shape (B) . Repeat the process making parallel stitches.

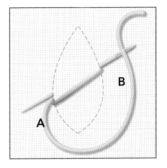

## Bullion Knots

To work a bullion knot, bring the needle up at one end of the stitch position. Take the needle back down into the fabric a thread away from the original stitch. Bring the needle back out 3 mm (1/8 in away from the original stitch, but don't pull the needle through the fabric entirely at this stage. Wrap the thread around the needle as many times as required (try 7 or 8 times to start with). Keeping the thread quite tight around the needle (hold it loosely), gently pull the needle through the fabric and the wrapped threads. Complete the knot by taking the needle back down into the fabric at the original start position. Increase the length of the stitch for more wraps or create a loop by wrapping extra times around the needle but only taking a short stitch.

## Bullion-knot Rose

To make a bullion-knot rose, use 3 strands of the darkest thread, stitch two bullion knots (7 wraps) side by side. To make the inner petals, use the medium shade and surround the centre with three bullion knots (7 wraps), which slightly overlap each other. To make the outer petals, using the lightest shade. Begin on the right-hand side, work four overlapping bullion knots (7–8 wraps) around the sides and bottom of the inner petals. If needed, still using the lightest colour work 2 bullion knots (11 wraps) below the previous petals to give a rose-like shape.

## Lazy Daisy Stitch

To make this petal-shaped stitch, bring the needle to the front. Using a sewing-style stitch, insert the needle back through the same hole but don't pull the thread through. Push the needle out again and out again two or more threads away, catching the thread under the needle. Gently pull the needle through the fabric to shape the loop. Take the needle back through the fabric on the other side of the loop catching the thread in place. Use this stitch to make leaves or a whole flower when worked in a ring.

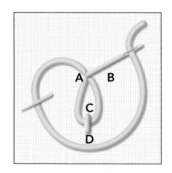

## Chain Stitch

Knot the thread. Bring the threaded needle through to the front of the fabric from the back (A).

Re-insert the needle tip into the fabric close to the point where it came out of the fabric (B).

Bring the needle point back out of the fabric a short distance from where it went in (C).

Wrap the thread under the point of the needle and pull the needle through the fabric maintaining a thread loop by not pulling the thread overly tight.

To continue chain stitching, insert the needle where it came out of the fabric, pointing down to the wrong side of the fabric. Bring the point of the needle back out of the fabric the same distance a you did the first stitch.

Loop the thread around the needle point.

Pull the needle through the fabric, as before maintaining the loop by not pulling the thread too tightly.

To finish the stitch, Insert the point of the

needle just on the outside of the thread loop so the thread will cover the end of the loop when it is tightened. Push the needle through to the back side of the fabric. Anchor the thread on the back of the fabric.

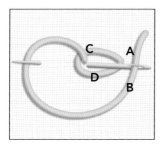

## WHIPPED CHAIN

The whipped chain is a decorative rope-like stitch which consists of a line of chain stitch which has been whipped on the surface with another colour. French Knot

To make a French knot, bring your needle up in the place where you wish to make the stitch. Wrap the thread around the needle twice and insert the needle back into the fabric close to the area where it was brought through. You should be able to easily slide the needle through the wrapped thread and down into the fabric. If you need to force the needle through the thread, or you knot pulls to the wrong side of the work your wrapping is too tight.

## MATTRESS STITCH

Locate the first bar in between the edge column of stitches and the next column.

Pick up that bar using a threaded tapestry needle. Arrange the second knitted piece next to the first. Locate the first bar next to the edge column in the second knitted piece, and pick up that bar with the needle.

**Note**: The needle will always be pointing in the direction that you are stitching: towards the end of the seam.

Pull the yarn through and pick up the next bar on the first knitted piece. Be sure to stay in the same column of bars, don't jump from one column to another. Pull yarn through firmly.

Find the next bar in the same column on the second piece and pick that up with your needle

Continue in this manner, alternating sides, staying in the same column of bars on each piece.

When pulling the yarn through, pull it firmly enough to bring the columns of stitches together, but not so firmly that the fabric puckers. On the first few stitches, it may help to pull on both ends of the seaming yarn.

Adjust the tension by gently tugging on the seaming yarn, and then on the fabric to get the beginning of the seam to lay flat.

Continue stitching, gently pulling each stitch so that the columns meet at the seam line.

The seam should be practically invisible.

# Pink Day Lily

This beautiful pink day lily flower brooch looks wonderful pinned to a winter coat. The flower is made from a square of knitted yarn, which is felted, then decorated with needle-felting and beadwork. The addition of freehand embroidery on the large petals ensures that no two lilies will ever be the same.

**Size**
18 cm (7 in) diameter

**Materials**
1 x 50 g (2 oz) ball of Wash+Filz-It! pink felting yarn
Pair of 5 mm (US 8) knitting needles
20 x 20 cm (8 x 8 in) pink wool felt, for backing
Small amounts of pink, purple and cream merino needle-felting wool
Needle felting needle
Small glass beads, bright pink and pale pink
6 pale pink glass beads each 4 mm (⅛ in)
Brooch back, 3 cm (1¼ in)
Beading needle
Sewing needle
Matching thread
Stranded embroidery cotton, dark crimson and medium pink
Foam block
Pink polyester thread

# FLOWER BROOCH

**1** Knit and felt the pink yarn according to the manufacturer's instructions. Allow to dry.

**2** Cut 6 large petals from pink felt and the same from pink wool felt for backing the petals. Cut six small petals from pink wool felt. Cut one circle 5 cm (2 in) diameter from pink felt for the brooch back.

**3** Needle-felt the large petals with a mixture of pink, purple and cream merino wool strands. Create a swirling design. For best effects, do not place too much yarn on the petal at once. Needle felt the small petals with pink needle-felting yarn only.

**4** Work chain stitch close to the outer edge of the large petals with dark crimson stranded embroidery cotton, and then whip the chain stitch with medium pink stranded embroidery cotton.

**5** With dark crimson stitch a wiggly line up the centre of each large petal using either back stitch or stem stitch. Sew a 4 mm pale glass bead to the top of each petal approximately 1 cm (3/8 in) down from the tip.

**6** Take the small inner petals, matching thread and beading needle and stitch two rows of bright pink glass beads along the bottom edge and then four rows of pale pink beads above these. Follow the shaping of the petal.

**7** Using a mixture of pink and purple merino needle-felting yarn, roll a ball the size of a large cherry between your palms for the flower centre. Place on the foam block and needle-felt into a firm shape. Add more yarn, if needed. Set aside.

**8** Using matching thread, stitch the inner petals together at their lower edges to form a circle. Run a gathering thread below the bottom row of bright pink beads and pull up to fit the felted ball. Pin to the felted ball, ensuring that most of the ball is protruding through the petals. Stitch in place through the ball and the petals.

**9** Take the large petal backs and stitch to the petal fronts with wrong sides together, using matching thread and taking very small stitches.

## To Make Up

Sew the large petals together right sides facing for 1.5 cm (½ in). Place the smaller flower in the centre. Stitch through all layers around the felted ball. Using medium pink, blanket stitch all round the 5 cm (2 in) diameter circle for the brooch back. Stitch the 3 cm (1¼ in) brooch back to the centre of the circle using. Sew to the back of the flower using small invisible stitches.

# Raspberry Sorbet Fingerless Gloves

These soft fingerless gloves are knitted in pale pink angora and have a delicate frill of raspberry mohair. This is a simple pattern with no difficult thumb shaping so novice knitters will be able to attempt it with confidence.

## Size
Small to medium
Length: 22 cm (8¾ in)

## Materials
1 x 25 g (1 oz) ball Rowan Kidsilk Haze, raspberry
2 x 10 g (½ oz) balls angora DK (8-ply), pale pink
Pair of 4 mm (US 6) knitting needles
Wool needle, for sewing up
3 mm (US 11) crochet hook
1 m (1 yd) x 1 cm (⅜ in)-wide velvet ribbon, dark pink

## Make 2

Using 4 mm knitting needles and raspberry yarn, cast on 176 sts.

**Row 1**: Purl.

**Row 2**: K2tog all across.

**Row 3**: Purl.

**Row 4**: K2tog all across.

**Row 5**: Purl (44 sts).

Change to pale pink.

**Row 1**: Knit.

**Row 2**: Purl.

**Row 3**: K1, *yfwd, k2tog, rep from * to last st, K1.

**Row 4**: Purl.

Work in K1, P1 rib for 8 rows.

**Next row**: *K1, sl l, K1, yfwd, psso (both sts), K1, rep from * to end of row.

**Next row**: Purl.

Rep these 2 rows until patt measures 13 cm (5 in) ending with a purl row.

Work another 6 rows of K1, P1 rib.

Break off pale pink and change to raspberry.

Work 2 rows st st.

**Next row**: Inc in every st.

**Next row**: Purl.

**Next row**: * K1, inc in next st, rep from * to last st, K1.

Cast off.

## To Make Up

Sew up the first 12 cm (4¾ in) of the side seam and last 6 rows of rib. Insert ribbon through eyelet holes and tie in a bow.

With raspberry and 3 mm crochet hook work a row of dc around thumb opening. Sew in all ends.

# Baby Socks

Socks are a useful and quick gift to make for a newborn baby and what could be prettier than a gift of seven pairs each in a different hue? These socks stay on little feet better than bootees.

### Size
To fit: 3–9 months
Length of foot: 8 cm (3¼ in)
    (can be adjusted, as desired)

### Materials
1 x 50 g ball 4-ply Shepherd
    Baby Wool Merino
Set of 4 x 2.25 mm (US 1)
    double-pointed knitting
    needles
Wool needle, for grafting toe

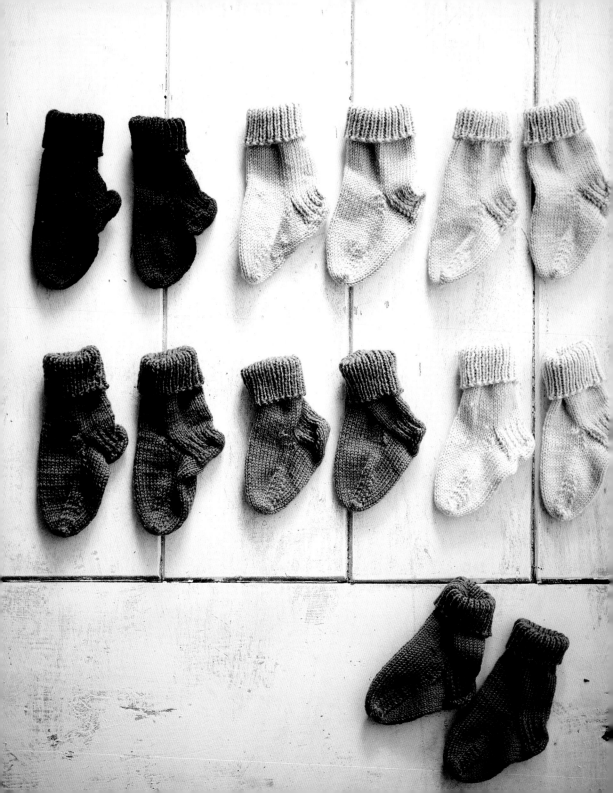

# SOCKS

Using set of 2.25 mm double-pointed knitting needles, cast on 40 sts (14, 12, 14). Join into a ring being careful not to twist sts.

Work 20 rounds K1, P1 rib. Cont in st st (every round knit) for another 20 rounds.

## Divide for Heel

**Next round**: K10, slip last sts from third onto same needle (20 sts for heel)

Divide rem sts between two needles.

**Note**: Heel sts are worked backwards and forwards in rows.

**Row 1**: Sl 1, P to end.

**Row 2**: *Sl 1, K1, rep from * to last st, K1.

Rep these two rows four times and then first row once.

## Turn Heel

**Next row**: K13, turn, P6, p2tog, turn, K7, k2tog, turn, K7, k2tog, turn, P7, p2tog, turn, K7, k2tog, turn, P7, p2tog, turn, K7, k2tog, turn, P7, p2tog, turn, K7, k2tog, turn, P7, p2tog (8 sts).

Place instep sts back on one needle.

**Next row**: Commencing at side of heel, pick up and K9 sts along side of heel. On next needle, knit instep sts. On next needle pick up and K9 sts along other side of heel, knit rem 4 heel st. Knitting is now back in the round (13 sts on first and third needles, 20 sts on second needle).

**Next round**: Knit.

**Next round**: First needle, Knit to last 3 sts, k2tog, K1; Second needle, Knit; Third needle, K1, sl 1, K1, psso, knit to end.

Rep these two rounds until 10 sts rem on first and third needles and 20 sts rem on second needle.

Work another 12 rounds without shaping.

## Shape Toe

**Next round**: Knit.

**Next round**: First needle, K to last 3 sts, k2tog, K1; Second needle, K1, sl 1, K1, psso, K to last 3 sts, k2tog, K1; Third needle, K1, sl 1, K1, psso, knit to end.

Rep these two rounds until 4 sts rem on first and third needle and 8 sts rem on second needle.

Knit sts from third needle onto first needle, then holding needles parallel graft rem toe sts together.

# Chicken Brooch

Knitted in 4-ply on very small needles, this chicken is quick to knit and because it is so small makes a great gift. Children love to hold these knitted birds. Find a brown variegated sock yarn: a 50 g (2 oz) ball will give you a whole flock of 30 multi-coloured chickens.

### Size
5 x 3 cm (2 x 1¼ in)

### Materials
Small amount of Regia Hand-Dye Effects 4-ply, brown shades
Small amount of 4-ply, black (for eyes), red (for comb), and yellow, (for beak)
Pair of 2 mm (US 0) knitting needles
2 x 2.75 mm (US 2) double-pointed knitting needles
Polyester fibre filling
Brooch back, 3 cm (1¼ in) long
Sewing needle
Matching thread

Using 2 mm knitting needles and Regia 4-ply, cast on 25 sts.

**Row 1**: Purl.

**Row 2**: K1, m1, K9, k2tog, K1, sl 1, K1, psso, K9, m1, K1.

**Row 3**: Purl.

Repeat rows 2 and 3 twice more.

**Row 8**: K1, m1, K23, m1, K1.

Commencing with a purl row, work 5 rows st st.

**Row 14**: K12, m1, K3, m1, K12.

**Row 15**: Purl.

**Row 16**: K13, m1, K3, m1, K13.

**Row 17**: Purl.

**Row 18**: K1, sl 1, psso (5 times), K4, m1, K3, m1, K4, k2tog (5 times).

**Row 19**: Purl.

**Row 20**: K1, sl 1, psso (3 times), K4, m1, K3, m1, K4, k2tog (3 times).

**Row 21**: Cast off 4 sts, purl to end.

**Row 22**: Cast off 4 sts, K3, m1, K3, m1, K4.

**Row 23**: Purl.

**Row 24**: Knit.

**Row 25**: P1, *p2tog, rep from * to end.

Break off yarn thread through rem sts, pull up tightly and fasten off.

**Note**: Garter st side is right side.

Sew up the centre seam, which will form the tummy, stuffing the body firmly as you go.

# WINGS
## Make 2

Using 2 mm knitting needles and Regia 4-ply, cast on 11 sts. Work in garter st throughout. Knit 3 rows.

### Begin Wing Shaping

**Next row**: K1, sl 1, K1, psso, K to end.

Repeat this row until 3 sts rem.

Break off yarn, thread through rem sts, pull up tightly and fasten off.

Fold wing in half and stitch closed. Place one wing on each side of chicken and stitch in place. The wide end of the wing faces the rear end of the chicken.

# BEAK AND CREST

Using a small amount of yellow 4-ply, embroider the beak using a few short stitches.

To make the crest, take a length of red 4-ply yarn and make a straight stitch on top of the head. Take a few stitches around this straight stitch to give a slightly curly effect.

To make the eyes, using black yarn, make a French knot on each side of the head. Take yarn back through the body and fasten off invisibly.

Sew brooch back along the bottom edge of wing. If you would prefer your chicken to sit flatter against any garment make the chicken with one wing and place the brooch where the wing would have been sewn.

# Appliqué Cot Blanket

This sweet little blanket is simple to make using just knit and purl stitches. The bold, bright square patches are decorated with fabric hearts, which are appliquéd in position. The piece is lined with soft fabric, for added comfort and warmth.

### Size
95 x 80 cm (37½ x 31½ in)
(each square measures
15 x 12.5 cm/37 x 31 in)

### Tension
28 sts and 36 rows to 10 cm
(4 in) square knitted on
3.75 mm (US 5) needles

### Materials
3 x 50 g balls Paton's Serenity
DK (8-ply) cotton mix, navy
3 x 50 g (2 oz) balls Paton's
Serenity, mid blue
3 x 50 g (2 oz) balls Paton's
Serenity, red

3 x 50 g (2 oz) balls Paton's
Serenity, green
1 pair 3.75 mm (US 5) knitting
needles
0.5 m (½ yd) iron-on interfacing
Iron
5 fat quarters for heart
appliqués
Sewing machine
Sewing cotton
Wool needle, for sewing
patches together
110 x 90 cm (43 x 35 in)
backing fabric
Thin card (card stock)
Pencil

# KNITTED SQUARES

**Make 35**: 9 each of navy, light blue and red, 6 green and 2 striped

Using 3.75 mm (US 5) knitting needles, cast on 40 sts.

Knit 6 rows garter stitch (every row knit).

**Row 7**: Knit.

**Row 8**: K4, purl to last 4 sts, K4.

Repeat rows 7 and 8 17 times more (36 rows in total).

Knit 6 rows garter st.

Cast off.

Make 2 striped squares by knitting 6 rows of garter stitch in navy, then 4 rows st st in alternating colours until row 36 is reached. Knit 6 rows of navy garter stitch. Darn in all ends. Press patches gently with warm iron, if needed.

## To Make Up

**1** Trace the heart template provided onto thin card and cut out. Fuse iron-on interfacing to the wrong side of the fat quarters using a hot iron and protecting the iron and ironing board. Draw around the heart on the interfacing to make 17 hearts in different colours. Satin stitch around each heart using the sewing machine, then cut out each heart. Alternatively, cut out each heart and then satin stitch the raw edges.

**2** Stitch the hearts in place on the knitted squares. Be careful not to stretch the squares.

**3** Arrange the squares using the diagram as a guide to colour. The white squares represent the striped patches. Using mattress stitch, sew the patches into rows. Join the rows together.

**4** Trim the backing fabric to the same dimensions as the blanket allowing extra all around to turn a double hem. Turn in, press and stitch a double hem all around.

**5** Place the blanket on top of the backing fabric wrong sides together. Sew the blanket to the backing, keeping the work flat as you go. Press lightly with a warm iron.

# Beautiful Buttons Handmade Card

This handmade card is made using felting and embroidery and is topped with a beautiful button. The lucky recipient could easily transform it into a brooch by removing it from the card and sewing a brooch back on to it.

## Materials

10 cm (4 in) square piece of dark grey felt

10 cm (4 in) square purple felt

10 cm (4 in) square aqua felt

1 x rectangular window card and envelope, 11 x 15 cm (4½ x 6 in)

1 piece of thin cardboard 13 x 9 cm (5 x 3¼ in) (this will be covered with the knitted piece)

1 x 50 g (2 oz) ball of Morris Avalon 4-ply Cotton, pale purple

1 x 3 cm (1¼ in) floral wooden button

Pair 3 mm (US 2/3) knitting needles

Double-sided tape

Stranded embroidery cotton, green, light blue, bright blue, violet

Embroidery needle

Chalk pencil

Using 3 mm knitting needles and 4-ply cotton, cast on 36 sts.

Work 2 rows garter st.

Cont in st st for 31 rows, ending with a knit row.

Knit 2 rows.

Cast off. Darn in all ends.

Use the double-sided tape to attach the knitted piece to the card.

## Embroidery

From dark grey felt cut one circle 6 cm (2¼ in) diameter. From purple felt cut one circle 5 cm (2 in) diameter. From aqua felt cut one circle 4 cm (1¾ in) diameter.

Use 3 strands of embroidery cotton throughout.

**1** Work a row of mauve around the outside of the grey felted circle.

**2** Place the purple felt circle and the aqua circle on top of the grey circle and secure with a few stitches.

**3** Place the button in the centre of the circle and use a chalk pencil to draw eight evenly spaced lines radiating out from the button and ending at the chain stitch.

**4** Work these eight radiating lines in three strands of bright blue embroidery cotton.

**5** With green, work a line of chain stitch around the aqua felt circle.

**6** Using light blue, make a 22-wrap bullion knot formed into a circle in each purple segment created by the stem stitch lines.

**7** Sew on the button with green embroidery cotton.

**8** Use double-sided tape to attach the button to the knitted fabric (so you can remove it if you want to turn it into a brooch) and more double-sided tape to attach the knitted card to the inside of the window card.

# Little Red Riding Hood Greetings Card

A lovely hand-painted button shaped like the heroine and some glass beads are put to good effect on this pretty greetings card. The button could have a brooch back attached afterwards and be worn as a very cute brooch.

## Measurements

11 x 15 cm (4¼ x 6 in)

## Materials

1 rectangular window card and envelope, 11 x 15 cm (4¼ x 6 in)

1 piece of thin card 13 x 9 cm (5 x 3½ in) (this will be covered with the knitted piece)

1 x 50 g (2 oz) ball of Morris Avalon 4-ply Cotton, white

1 x 4.5 cm (1¾ in) Little Red Riding Hood wooden button

Pair 3 mm (US 2/3) knitting needles

Double-sided tape

Stranded embroidery cotton, red

Embroidery needle

Chalk pencil

Glass beads, red

Beading needle

# GREETING CARD

Using 3 mm knitting needles and 4-ply cotton,
cast on 36 sts. Work 2 rows garter st. Cont in
st st (one row knit, one row purl) for 31 rows,
ending with a knit row.

Knit 2 rows.

Cast off. Darn in all ends.

Work a row of chain stitch, 9 rows up and
9 rows down from the top and bottom, using
three strands of red embroidery cotton.

Stitch the red riding hood button to the
centre. Sew the red glass beads randomly but
evenly around the button and between the red
embroidered lines.

Use the double-sided tape to attach the knitted
piece to the card.

And more double sided tape to attach the
knitted card to the inside of the window card.

# Lavender Bags

These pretty moss stitch lavender bags are just the thing to keep clothes sweetly scented while they hang in the closet; the dried lavender flowerheads kept inside will also repel any insects that might damage clothing. They fun bags are quick to make and can be decorated with an assortment of favourite embellishments.

**Measurements** 10 x 9 cm
(4 x 3½ in)

**Materials**
Oddments of DK (8-ply) cotton
Stranded embroidery cotton, light, medium and dark, for bullion rose; green for leaves
30 cm (12 in) narrow ribbon, for each bag
4 or 5 fancy beads, each 1 cm (⅜ in) diameter
Selection of buttons, each 1 cm (⅜ in) diameter or less
Small glass beads
Sewing thread
Sewing needle
Beading needle
Wool needle
Dried lavender flowerheads, approximately 40 g (1½ oz) per bag
Pair of 3.25 mm (US 3) knitting needles

# LAVENDER BAG

Using 3.25 mm knitting needles and DK (8-ply) cotton, cast on 23 sts.

**Row 1**: *K1, P1, rep from * to last st ending with K1.

**Row 2**: As row 1.

Rep these 2 rows until work measures 23 cm (9 in). Cast off.

## FOR EMBROIDERED LAVENDER BAG

Stitch 9 or 10 bullion-knot roses and space them evenly over the surface of the moss st knitting.

Using 3 strands of green embroidery cotton, work pairs of lazy daisy stitch around the roses. Thread a beading needle with sewing thread and secure firmly at the back of the work. Stitch small glass beads around the roses and leaves.

### To Make Up

**1** Fold the knitted piece in half with right sides together and cast on and cast off edges aligned. Stitch together one short edge and the long edge. Turn right side out.

**2** Thread 4 or 5 fancy glass beads on to a doubled length of sewing thread (use beading thread for added strength if you like). Add a small glass bead to the end then bring the needle back up through the fancy glass beads. Stitch this string of beads very firmly half way along the short stitched edge of the lavender bag to create a fringe at the bottom edge. Secure with a knot inside the bag.

**3** Fold the ribbon length into a loop. Sew this to the inside of the centre seam. It will be hidden when you stitch the top closed.

**4** Three-quarters fill the bag with lavender flowerheads. Close the top seam to form a triangular shape, the back seam will now be running down the centre. Stitch firmly closed.

## FOR BUTTON LAVENDER BAGS

Arrange the buttons across the knitted piece and then stitch in place. Sew glass beads on in the same way.

# Summer Cotton Baby Hat

Here is a lovely cotton hat with a wide brim to keep the sun off tender baby skin. Lined with lightweight floral fabric and decorated with a matching bow this will make a great addition to any new baby's wardrobe. It is quick to make in doubled 4-ply cotton. The brim lining is made in soft, lightweight fabric.

### Size
To fit: 3, (6, 12) months

### Materials
2 x 50 g (2 oz) balls Heirloom
   Cotton 4-ply, white
Pair of 4 mm (US 6) knitting
   needles
Pair of 3.25 mm (US 3) knitting
   needles
Wool needle, for sewing in
   ends
0.5 m (½ yd) lightweight floral
   fabric for brim lining and
   bow

Fabric marker
Sewing machine (Optional)
Fabric scissors
Matching thread
Sewing needle

# HAT

Using 4 mm knitting needles and yarn held double, cast on 82, (90, 96) sts.

Work 3 rows garter st, inc 8 (8, 10) sts evenly across last row (90, 98,106) sts.

Beg with a knit row, work 16, (18, 20) rows st st, inc 0, (1, 2) sts evenly across last row (90, 99, 108) sts.

## SHAPE CROWN

**Row 1**: *K8, (9, 10), k2tog, rep from * to end.

**Row 2** and alt rows: Purl.

**Row 3**: *K7, (8, 9), k2tog, rep from * to end.

**Row 5**: *K6, (7, 8), k2tog, rep from * to end.

**Row 7**: *K5, (6, 7), k2tog, rep from * to end.

**Row 9**: *K4, (5, 6), k2tog, rep from * to end.

Cont to dec in this manner in alt rows until 9 sts rem.

Break off yarn, thread through rem sts, pull up tightly and fasten off.

## BRIM

Using 3.25 mm knitting needles and Heirloom Cotton 4-ply held double, cast on 12, (13, 14) sts.

**Note**: When making turnings, bring yarn to the front of work, slip next st on to right-hand needle, yarn back, slip st back on to left-hand needle, turn and proceed as instructions. This avoids creating holes in the work.

**Row 1**: Knit to last 4 sts, turn.

**Row 2**: Knit to end.

**Row 3**: Knit.

**Row 4**: Knit.

These 4 rows form patt. Cont in patt until brim fits around the base of the hat, ending on a third row. You will have made a circle shape. Cast off.

### Lining the Brim

**1** Fold the lining in half, selvedges together.

**2** Fold the brim piece in half so that it is a semi-circle shape. Place the brim on top of the lining, positioning it on the bias (diagonally across the warp and weft threads), so that the fabric will have some stretch and make it easier to hem as well as to attach to the knitted fabric.

**3** Using a fabric marker, draw around brim. Cut out adding a 1 cm (³/₈ in) seam allowance all around.

**4** With right sides together sew the two straight edges of the semi-circles together to form a circle, using 1 cm (³/₈ in) seam allowance. Trim the seam and bind the raw edges with a zigzag stitch.

**5** Bind the raw outer edges of the brim with zigzag stitch in the same way. This makes it easier to hem. If your machine has a rolled hem foot, use this to hem the outer edge of the brim. If not, fold a very narrow double hem all the way around and hand or machine stitch in place.

**6** With wrong sides together place fabric brim on top of knitted brim. Check for fit and trim the inner edge if necessary. Once you are happy that both pieces match, bind the inner edge of the lining with zigzag stitch or turn in a very narrow hem and stitch in place. Pin in place, matching centre back seam with a lining seam and use plenty of pins for a smooth finish. Using a blind hemming stitch, sew the outer edges together.

**7** Stitch the inner edge to the inner knitted edge using small stitches.

**8** Pin the crown and brim together, right sides facing, matching back seam of brim and centre back seam of crown. The garter stitch rows on the crown make a good guide to stitch around. Stitch in place with small stitches.

**9** Fold the centre of the front of the hat brim up and catch in place with stitches through brim and hat.

## Fabric Bow

**1** Cut a 12 cm (4¾ in) square of floral fabric for the bow. Fold in half with right sides together and stitch all the way around leaving a small opening for turning. Turn right side out, press the corners out, stitch the opening closed and iron flat. Topstitch around the outer edge. Fold in half along the long edge and press lightly to mark.

**2** For the central tie, cut another piece of floral fabric 5 x 9 cm (2 x 3½ in). Turn in a hem on the short ends and one long end. Beginning at the raw edge, fold the fabric into thirds. Stitch along the long edge so piece is now folded in three with one short edge hemmed and the long edge stitched closed.

**3** Tightly wrap the tie around the middle of the bow so that the bow fabric gathers tightly together at its centre. Pin and stitch in place right through the bow, ensuring that it is firm. Sew to the front centre of the turned up brim.

# Watercolour Leaf Brooch

Perfect to add colour and interest to an autumnal outfit, this brooch makes use of several techniques. First felting yarn is knitted into a square. It is then washed so that the strands of yarn felt together. Once dry, the resulting fabric is cut to shape and then decorated with needle felting and embroidery.

### Size
*Large leaf*
12 cm (4¾ in) long

*Small leaf*
5 cm (2 in) long

### Materials
1 x 50 g (2 oz) ball of Wash+Filz-It! dark grey felting yarn
Pair of 5 mm (US ) knitting needles
Brooch back, 3 cm (1¼ in) long
Needle-felting needle
Small amounts of needle-felting merino wool in dark blue, green, bright green, purple, bright aqua
Sewing thread, dark grey
Stranded embroidery cotton in mauve, dark blue, dark mauve, gold
Embroidery needle
Sewing needle

1 Knit and felt the dark grey yarn according to the instructions on the yarn label.

2 Felt the fabric according to the manufacturer's instructions. Allow to dry.

3 Cut out one large and one small leaf using the templates provided.

4 Cut one piece 4 x 3 cm (1¾ x 1¼ in) for attaching the brooch back. Stitch the brooch back to the 4 x 3 cm (1¾ x 1¼ in) piece using matching thread.

5 Lightly needle felt the large and small leaves all over using a mixture of the colours. For best effects place the strands of merino felting yarn very lightly on top of each other and then needle felt. This works better than working one colour at a time.

6 Using three strands of embroidery cotton, work a row of chain stitch 0.5 cm (¼ in) from the edge of the large and small leaves. Whip the large leaf using short lengths of gold thread (it tends to unravel or knot very easily). Whip the small leaf chain st in dark blue.

7 Along the lower edge of the leaf work eight semi-circles using dark mauve stem stitch.

8 Inside each semi-circle work a three 20-wrap bullion knots using dark mauve.

9 In the centre of the bullion knot loop work a French knot in gold thread.

10 In the centre of the small leaf work nine French knots in gold thread.

11 In the centre of the large leaf work the centre veins in three strands of dark blue embroidery cotton. As the small leaf will cover a lot of the large leaf you only need to work the side veins near the top of the leaf.

12 Place the small leaf on top of the large leaf in the lower half and stitch firmly in place.

13 On the wrong side sew the brooch back piece in place using matching thread and a sewing needle.

# Poppy Brooch

Give a favourite dark-toned outfit a splash of colour with this vibrant poppy brooch. Made for knitted and felted fabric, the surface is needle-felted and machine embroidered.

**Size**
8 cm (3 in) in diameter

**Materials**
1 x 50 g (2 oz) ball of Wash+Filz-It! red felting yarn
Pair of 5 mm (US 8 ) knitting needles
15 cm (6 in)square of black felt
Frosted black beads
Stranded embroidery cottons, black and red
3 cm (1¼ in) brooch back
Sewing threads, red and black
Sewing needle
Beading needle
Small handful of merino needle felting wool, red or black
Needle-felting needle
Foam block

# POPPY BROOCH

1 Knit and felt the red yarn following the instructions on the yarn label.

2 Felt the fabric according to the manufacturer's instructions. Allow to dry.

3 Cut 1 backing piece from black felt using the template provided.

4 Cut five petals from red knitted and felted fabric using the template provided.

5 Cut 1 round black centre using the template provided.

6 Sew the petals together at their sides using matching thread and ladder stitch. Use very small stitches and ensure your work is firmly held together. Set aside.

7 Take some of the needle-felting yarn and shape into a ball. Needle felt until it is the size of a large pea by stabbing it repeatedly with the needle until it is nice and firm. Always work on a protected surface so that there is no danger that you will stab yourself with the needle.

8 Sew a gathering stitch 0.5 cm (¼ in) the inside edge of the black felt circle using black thread. Pull up the gathers and place the felted ball inside so that the ball is firmly encased. This will be the flower centre. Fasten off tightly.

9 Cover the black ball with frosted black glass beads, sewing each on one at a time.

10 Place the bead-covered ball through the centre of the five petal flower and stitch firmly in place.

11 Using three strands of black embroidery cotton, on each petal work 2 or 3 stem-stitch stamens, each 1 cm (³/₈ in) long. On top of each stamen work a 20-wrap bullion knot.

12 Place the poppy front and back wrong sides together, and blanket stitch all the way around using two strands of red embroidery cotton. Trim the black felt to fit the poppy, if necessary. Sew on the brooch back.

# Bluebell Coat and Hat Set

The little coat is knitted in garter stitch and mostly in one piece. Just the collar and lace edging are knitted separately. Similarly, the hat is knitted on two needles and then the lace band is sewn on at completion. The little bullion roses add a delicate touch.

## Size

*Coat*
To fit: 0–3 months, 6–9 months
Length to back of neck:
  25, (27) cm/10, (11) in
Sleeve length with cuff not
  folded back 16 (18) cm/
  6 ¼, (7) in

*Hat*
33 (35.5) cm/13, (14) in
  diameter

## Materials
3 (3) x 50 g (2 oz) balls
  Shepherd Baby Wool Merino
  4-ply, shade 2935, blue
Pair of 3.25 mm (US 3) knitting
  needles
Pair of 3 mm (US 2/3) knitting
  needles
Stitch holder
2 x 2.25 mm (US 1) double-
  pointed knitting needles
4 x 1 cm (⅜ in) diameter
  matching buttons
Matching sewing thread
Stranded embroidery cotton
  in yellow, pale blue, medium
  blue and bright green
Wool needle
Embroidery needle

## Tension
26 sts and 46 rows to 10 cm
  (4 in) square when measured
  over garter st on 3.25 mm
  (US 3) needles.

# COAT

Using 3.25 mm knitting needles and 4-ply yarn, cast on 53 (59) sts. Work in garter st until work measures 11.5 (14) cm/4½, (5½) in.

**Next row**: (RS) K53 (59) sts, cast on 42 (46) for first sleeve (95, 105 sts).

**Next row**: K95 (105) sts, cast on 42 (46) sts for second sleeve (137, 151 sts).

Cont is garter st until sleeve section measures 8.5 (9) cm from cast on sts ending with a WS row. Work now measures 20 (23) cm/8 (9) in from beg.

## SHAPE NECK

**Next row**: K58 (64) sts and leave these sts on st holder for right front and sleeve. Cast off 21, (23) sts for back of neck, with 1 st already on needle, knit rem 57 (63) sts.

Complete left sleeve and left front as follows:

**Next row**: K58 (64) sts, turn.

Cont in garter st on these sts for 2 (2) cm (¾ in) ending with a RS row (end at sleeve cuff edge).

**Next row**: (WS) K58 (64) sts, cast on 16 (17) sts (74, 81 sts). Work another 8 rows garter st.

## FOR GIRLS' VERSION

Cont in garter st until sleeve measures 17 (18) cm/6½ (7) in from cast-on edge, ending with a RS row.

**Next row**: (WS) Cast off 42 (46) sts, knit to end. Cont in garter st on rem sts until left front measures 20 (23) cm/8 (9) in from back neck cast-off, ending with a WS row (make sure to end with the same number of garter st ridges as on back from cast-on to beg of sleeve). Front and back are the same length when the sleeve is folded in half. Cast off.

## FOR BOYS' VERSION

**Next row**: (RS) make first buttonhole: K4, k2tog, yon, knit to end of row.

Cont in garter st for another 4 (3.5) cm/(1½ (1¼) in.

Make second buttonhole as for first.

Continue in garter st until sleeve measures 17 (18) cm/6½ (7) in from cast-on edge, ending with a RS row.

**Next row**: (WS) Cast of 42 (46) sts, knit to end of row. Cont in garter st for rem of left front and make 2 (3) more buttonholes as above, every 4 (3.5) cm/1½ (1¼) in.

Cont in garter st until front measures 20 (23) cm/8 (9) in from back neck cast-off edge, ending with a WS row (make sure to end with the same number of garter st ridges as on back from cast on to beg of sleeve). Front and back are the same length when the sleeve is folded in half. Cast off.

## FOR BOTH VERSIONS

Complete right front and right sleeve.

Slip the sts from the stitch holder onto needle, making sure the first row will be a WS row.

**Next row**: (WS) K58 (64) sts. Turn.

Cont in garter st for 2 (2) cm/³⁄₄ (³⁄₄) in ending with a WS row at sleeve cuff.

**Next row**: (RS) K58 (64) sts, cast on 16 (17) sts (74, 81 sts). Work another 8 rows garter st.

## For Boys' Version

Cont in garter st until sleeve measures 17 (18) cm/6½ (7) in from cast-on edge, ending with a WS row.

**Next row**: (RS) Cast off 42 (46) sts, knit to end. Cont in garter st on rem sts for right front until front measures 20 (23) cm/8 (9) in from back neck cast-off, ending with a WS row (make sure to end with the same number of garter st ridges as on back from cast-on edge to beg of sleeve). Front and back are the same length when the sleeve is folded in half. Cast off.

## For Girls' Version

**Next row**: (WS) Make buttonhole: K4, k2tog, yon, knit to end of row.

Cont in garter st for another 4 (3.5) cm/1½ (1¼) in.

Make another buttonhole as for first.

Cont in garter st until sleeve measures 17 (18) cm/6½ (7) in from cast-on edge, ending with a RS row.

**Next row**: (WS) Cast off 42 (46) sts, knit to end of row. Cont in garter st for rem of left front and make 2 (3) more buttonholes as above, every

4 (3.5) cm. Cont in garter st until front measures 20 (23) cm/8 (9) in from back neck cast-off edge, ending with a WS row (make sure to end with the same number of garter st ridges as on back from cast on to beg of sleeve). Front and back are the same length when the sleeve is folded in half. Cast off.

## Collar

With WS facing, using 3.25 mm knitting needles and 4-ply yarn, beg 5 sts in from front neck edge, pick up and K11 (12) sts along front neck edge, 1 st at neck corner, 6 (6) sts along straight neck-shoulder edge, 21 (23) sts along back neck, 6 (7) sts down straight neck-shoulder edge, 1 st at neck corner, and 11 (12) sts along right front neck edge omitting last 5 sts of neck edge (57, 61 sts).

Work 6 rows garter st.

**Next row**: K11 (12) sts, inc in next st, K3, inc in next st, K2 (2) sts, inc in next st, K19 (21) sts, inc in next st, K2 (2) sts, inc in next st, K3, inc in next st, K11 (12) (63, 67 sts).

Cont in garter st without further shaping until collar measures 6 (7) cm/2½ (2¾) in from beg. Cast off.

## Lace Panel

This is a 10-row repeat. Make 1 lace panel to fit around the bottom of the coat when slightly stretched and another to fit around the lower

edge of the hat when slightly stretched.

Using 3 mm knitting needles and 4-ply yarn, cast on 8 sts.

Knit 1 row.

**Row 1**: Sl 1, K1, (yo, k2tog) twice, yo, K2.

**Rows 2, 4, 6 and 8**: Sl 1, knit to end of row.

**Row 3**: Sl 1, K2, (yo, K2tog) twice, yo, K2.

**Row 5**: Sl 1, K3, (yo, K2tog) twice, yo K2.

**Row 7**: Sl 1, K4, (yo, K2tog) twice, yo, K2.

**Row 9**: Sl 1, K11.

**Row 10**: Cast off 4 sts, knit to end of row.

Repeat rows 1–10 until piece is desired length, ending with a row 10.

## To Make Up

Sew sleeve and side seams using mattress st. Stitch lace panel in place to lower edge. Sew buttons on.

# HAT

Using 3.25 mm knitting needles and 4-ply yarn, cast on 77 (83) sts. Work in garter st until hat measures 12 (13) cm/4¾ (5) in from beg, ending with a WS row.

## Shape Crown

**Next row**: (RS) K6, sl 1, K1, psso, K2, k2tog, *K6 (7), sl 1, K1, psso, K2, k2tog, rep from * 4 times, K5 (6) (65, 71 sts).

Work 3 rows garter st.

**Next row**: (RS) K5, sl 1, K1, psso, K2, k2tog, *K4 (5), sl 1, K1, psso, K2, k2tog, rep from * 4 times, K4 (5) (53, 59 sts).

Work 3 rows garter st.

**Next row**: (RS) K4, sl 1, K1, psso, K2, k2tog, *K2 (3), sl 1, K1, psso, K2, k2tog, rep from * 4 times, K3 (4) (41, 47 sts).

Knit 1 row.

**Next row**: (RS) K3, sl 1, K1, psso, K2, k2tog, *K0 (1), sl 1, K1, psso, K2, k2tog, rep from * 4 times, K2 (3) (29, 35 sts).

Knit 1 row.

## Larger Size Only

**Next row**: K2, sl 1, K1, psso, K2, k2tog, *K1, sl 1, K1, psso, K2, k2tog, rep from * four times, K2 (33 sts).

Knit 1 row.

## Both Sizes

K2tog all across, ending with K1 (15, 18 sts). Break off yarn, thread through rem sts, pull up tightly and fasten off.

## Lace Panel

Make a lace panel, as for jacket to fit around lower edge of hat.

## To Make Up

With RS together, stitch lace panel to lower edge of hat, then with RS together sew centre back seam of hat.

## LOOP FOR TOP OF HAT

Using 2 x 2.25 mm double-pointed knitting
needles and 4-ply yarn, cast on 3 sts. Work an
I-cord for 6 cm (2½ in).
**Next row**: Sl 1, k2tog, psso. Fasten off.
Attach to the top of the hat securely.

# EMBROIDERY

**1** Use three strands of embroidery cotton
throughout. Embroider seven bullion roses
around the base of the hat. Use the darker shade
for the centre knot and the paler colour for the
outer petals.

**2** Make a green French knot to each side of
the rose.

**3** On the coat embroider a blue bullion rose at
each corner of the collar, each with a French
knot at both sides of the rose.

**4** Embroider 10 bullion roses along the lower
lace panel, alternating yellow and blue. There is a
green French knot on each side of each rose.

# Aquamarine Socks

Socks are one of the loveliest gifts a knitter can make. There are so many beautiful self-patterning sock yarns available and all produce a different effect. Practise the technique on some spare yarn first to make sure that the stitches are neat and even.

## Size
Ladies, to fit shoe size UK
  5–8/AUS 6–8/US 7½–10/
  EUR 38–41 (length can be
  adjusted)

## Materials
1 x 100 g (3½ oz) skein Lorna's
  Laces 4-ply Shepherd Sock
  Yarn, shade 92, river
4 x 2.25 mm (US 1) double-
  pointed knitting needles
Wool needle, for grafting toe

# SOCKS
## Make 2

Using 3 x 2.25 mm double-pointed knitting
needles and 4-ply sock yarn, cast on 72 sts (24,
24, 24). Join into a ring, being careful not to
twist sts.

Work in K2, P2 rib for 10 cm (4 in) for rib.

Work one round decreasing 2 stitches evenly
(70 stitches).

Work from graph, and beginning on row 1, work
seven pattern repeats across row.

Work 70 rows as set.

Graph symbols

0        yfwd

λ        Sl 1, K1, psso

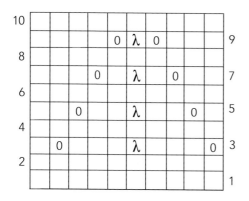

## Divide for Heel

**Note**: Heel is worked backwards and forwards
on two needles.

**Next row**: K18. Sl last 18 sts from needle 3
onto same needle. Divide rem sts between two
needles. Working on 36 stitches on needle 1 and
working backwards and forwards in rows.

**Row 1**: Sl 1, P to end of row.

**Row 2**: *Sl 1, K1, rep from * to last st, K1.

Rep these 2 rows 14 times and then row 1 once.

## Turn Heel

K22, turn, P10, turn, K9, sl 1, K1, psso, K1, turn,
P10, p2tog, P1, turn, K11, sl 1, K1, psso, K1, turn,
P12, p2tog, P1, turn, K13, sl 1, K1, psso, K1, turn,
P14, p2tog, P1, turn, cont in this manner until all
sts are worked onto one needle (22 sts).

Knit first 11 heel sts on to one needle. Place all
instep sts back on to one needle. Commencing
at centre of heel, K11, pick up and K17 sts down
side of heel flap, knit across instep sts, pick up
and K17 sts along other side of heel flap with
third needle and K rem 11 heel sts. Knitting is
now back in the round.

## Shape Instep

**Round 1**: Knit.

**Round 2**: Knit to last 4 sts, k2tog, K2. Knit across
instep sts on third needle, K2, sl 1, K1, psso, knit
to end of round.

Rep rounds 1 and 2 until 17 sts rem on needles
1, and 3 and 34 sts rem on needle 2.

Cont without further shaping until foot

measures 15 cm (6 in) from point where sts were picked up at side of heel. Socks can be made longer at this point, however you may need to purchase more yarn).

## SHAPE TOE

**Round 1**: Knit.

**Round 2**: First needle, knit to last 4 sts, k2tog, K2; Second needle, K2, sl 1, K1, psso, knit to last 4 sts, k2tog, K2; Third needle, K2, sl 1, K1, psso, knit to end of round.

Rep these two rounds until 7 sts rem on needle 1 and 3, and 14 sts rem on needle 2.

Knit one more round. Slide sts from needle 3 onto end of needle 1 so they are parallel to each other. Graft toe stitches together (see techniques).

# Men's Vintage-style Scarf

The basketweave pattern on this fabulous scarf is made up of combinations of plain knit and purl stitches – just keep a running record of the row that you've knitted, so you don't get confused when you pick it up after a break. The reversible colours are conservative making them ideal for a male recipient.

### Size
165 x 25 cm (65 x 10 in)

### Tension
28 sts and 30 rows of pattern to 10 cm (4 in) square when worked on 4 mm knitting needles

### Materials
6 x 50 g (2 oz) balls Rowan Belle Organic DK (8 ply), dark grey

1 x 50 g (2 oz) ball Rowan Belle Organic DK (8 ply), light grey
Pair of 4 mm (US 6) knitting needles
3 mm (US 2½) crochet hook
Wool needle, for sewing in ends
10 cm (4 in)-wide piece card (card stock) to wind fringe around

## SCARF

Using 4 mm knitting needles and dark grey, cast on 70 sts.

**Rows 1–3**: *K7, P7, repeat from * to end of row.

**Rows 4–6**: *K2, P3, K2, P2, K3, P2, rep from * to end of row.

**Rows 7–9**: *K7, P7, rep from * to end of row.

**Rows 10–12**: *P7, K7, rep from * to end of row.

**Rows 13–15**: *P2, K3, P2, K2, P3, K2, rep from * to end of row.

**Rows 16–18**: * P7, K7, rep from * to end of row.

These 18 rows form patt.

Break off dark grey and work 18-row pattern rep in light grey. Break off light grey and join dark grey. Continue in patt until scarf measures 140 cm (55 in) or length desired, ending with 18th row of pattern. Break off dark grey and join in light grey. Work 18 patt rows of light grey and then break off light grey and re-join dark grey and work another 18 patt rows of dark grey. Cast off.

## FRINGE

To make fringe, wrap yarn around the 10 cm (4 in)-wide cardboard strip. Try to keep the wraps vertical so that when you cut along one edge the fringing will all be the same length. You will need 70 dark and 70 light grey lengths. To attach to the end of the scarf, fold each in half and push the crochet hook through the cast-on loop, hook both ends of the yarn over the crochet hook and pull through to fasten off. Work along the cast-on edge alternating dark and light grey yarn. Then repeat the process with the other end of the scarf. Trim edge of fringe, if needed. Do NOT press this scarf.

# Covered Coat Hanger and Lavender Bag

Keep delicate clothes off the closet floor with this lovely covered padded hanger. The padding will ensure that fragile fabric is not marked. The accompanying felted, embroidered lavender bag makes clothes smell sweet.

## Size
***Lavender bag***: 9 x 9 cm (3½ x 3½ in)

## Materials
1 padded coat hanger
1 x 50 g (2 oz) ball of Sirdar Baby Bamboo, dark purple
Pair of 4 mm (US 6) knitting needles
Wool needle
Dried lavender flowerheads
Small amount of polyester fibre filling
30 x 2.5 cm (12 x 1 in)-wide ribbon, pink variegated

15 cm (16 in) square dark grey felt
Pair 5 mm (US 8) knitting needles
Stranded embroidery cotton: mauve, dark mauve, blue, bright yellow
Embroidery needle
Chalk pencil
Matching sewing thread
Sewing needle

# HANGER COVER

Using 4 mm knitting needles and dark purple, cast on 25 sts. Work in moss st.

**Row 1**: *K1, P1, rep from * to end.

Rep this row until work measures same length as coat hanger when slightly stretched. Cast off.

## To Make Up

Sew short ends together so that you have a long thin piece. Turn right side out. Unscrew the curved hanger section and set aside. Place the knitted piece over the padded hanger, mark with chalk pencil where the wire hanger will fit back in, and then bring the edges together underneath. Using mattress stitch, sew closed. Cover the wire hanger with ribbon, leave plain or cover with yarn using blanket stitch. Darn in any loose ends. Fit hook back on hanger.

# LAVENDER HEART

1 Cut 2 lavender hearts from grey felt using the template provided.

2 Mark the two large outer swirls with chalk pencil on the grey felt hearts, and using 3 strands of mauve embroidery cotton work two rows of stem stitch 3 mm ($^1/_8$ in) apart and tapering towards the point of the heart. Cover the stem stitch with satin stitch using 3 strands of mauve embroidery cotton.

3 Outline these 2 large swirls with stem stitch on both sides using 3 strands dark mauve embroidery cotton.

4 For the extra decorative detail, using 3 strands of blue embroidery cotton make a bullion knot loop with 25 wraps. Work 1 blue bullion knot loop at the halfway point of the heart on the outer edge of the large swirl on each side.

5 With right sides together join the heart using blanket stitch and 3 strands of bright yellow embroidery cotton. Leave an opening at the top for filling.

6 Fill with a mixture of dried lavender flowerheads and polyester fibre filling to give a nice plump shape.

7 Fold the ribbon in half and insert into the opening. Stitch in place with sewing thread and then continue the blanket stitch all around the opening. Hang the lavender bag over the coat hanger.

# Fabulous Fair Isle Children's Gloves

Perfect to help keep a young child warm on a cold winter's day, these gloves are knitted using a Fair Isle pattern. Don't be daunted if you have never knitted with this technique before, there are only two colours in any row. The gloves are knitted on two needles rather than in the round to make them easier.

### Size
To fit: 6–8 years old

### Materials
1 x 50 g (2 oz) ball 4-ply merino/possum blend, grey
1 x 50 g (2 oz) ball Jamiesons Spindrift 4-ply, dark purple
1 x 50 g (2 oz) ball Jamiesons Spindrift 4-ply, dark bright purple
1 x 50 g (2 oz) ball Jamiesons Spindrift 4-ply, damson
1 x 50 g (2 oz) ball Jamiesons Spindrift 4-ply, bright pink
1 x 50 g (2 oz) ball Jamiesons Spindrift 4-ply, light pink
Pair of 2.25 mm (US 1) knitting needles
3 mm (US 11) crochet hook
Wool needle, for sewing up

### Tension
32 sts and 42 rows to 10 cm (4 in) square worked over st st using 4-ply merino/possum blend
Tension needs to be quite firm. Be sure to sew up very firmly using small stitches.

## READING CHART

Read knit rows from right to left and purl rows from left to right. Be careful not to pull yarn tightly behind work. There will be a few ends to darn in when finishing but this is preferable to carrying the yarn up the sides, which will make the knitting very bulky.

## RIGHT-HAND GLOVE

Using 2.25 mm knitting needles and grey 4-ply yarn, cast on 54 sts.

**Row 1**: K1, P1 to end

**Row 2**: P1, K1 to end.

Continue in rib as set until 37 rows have been completed.

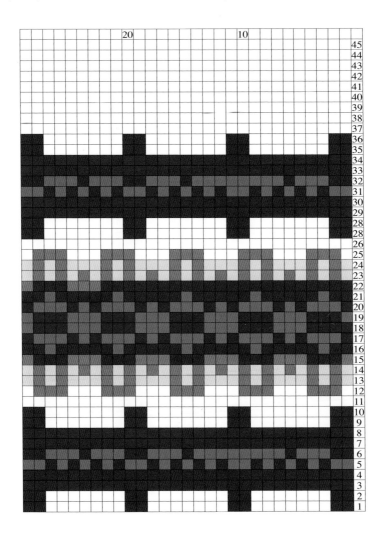

Work 4 rows st st.

## COMMENCE CHART

**Row 1**: Patt 29 from chart, K25 grey. Twist yarn together at point where two colours meet on each row so holes don't form.

**Row 2**: P25 grey, patt 29 from chart.

Rep these 2 rows twice.

**Row 7**: Commence increases for thumb gusset as follows; patt 29 from chart, then, using grey, K1, inc in next 2 sts, K22.

**Row 8**: Using grey, P to last 29 sts. Patt 29 from chart.

**Row 9**: Patt 29 from chart, K to end using grey.

**Row 10**: As row 8.

**Row 11**: Patt 29 from chart, then using grey, K1, inc in next st, K2, inc in next st, K to end.

Rep rows 8–11 five times, allowing for 2 extra sts in thumb gusset after each inc (68 sts).

**Next row**: Using grey, p to last 29 sts. Patt 29 from chart.

## COMMENCE THUMB

Patt 29 from graph, K17 using grey, turn and cast on 2 sts.

**Next row**: Using grey, P18, turn and cast on 2 sts. Work in st st on these 20 sts until thumb measures 4 cm (1½ in).

## SHAPE TOP OF THUMB

**Row 1**: *K1, k2tog, rep from * to last 2 sts, K2.

**Row 2**: Purl.

**Row 3**: *K2tog, rep from * to end.

Break off yarn, thread through rem sts, and pull up tightly. Fasten off securely, then sew down side of thumb to base.

With RS facing, using grey, pick up and K4 sts from base of thumb, knit to end of row.

**Next row**: Using grey, P to last 29 sts. Patt to end using chart. Continue in patt on these 29 sts, keeping the remaining sts grey st st until chart has been completed. Cont in grey for remainder of glove.

## FIRST FINGER

**Row 1**: K36, turn, cast on 1 st.

**Row 2**: P17, turn, cast on 1 st.

Continue in st st on these 18 sts until work measures 5 cm (2 in) ending with a purl row.

## Shape Top

**Row 1**: (K1, k2tog) 6 times.

**Row 2**: Purl.

**Row 3**: (K2tog) 6 times.

Break off yarn, complete as for thumb.

## SECOND FINGER

With RS facing, rejoin grey yarn and K2 sts from base of first finger, K7 from left-hand needle, turn and cast on 1 st.

**Next row**: P17 sts, turn and cast on 1 st.

Cont in st st on these 18 sts until work measures 6 cm (2¼ in), ending with a purl row.

Shape top and finish as for first finger.

## THIRD FINGER

With RS facing, rejoin grey yarn and K2 sts from base of second finger, K6, turn and cast on 1 st.

**Next row**: P15, turn and cast on 1 st.

Continue on these 16 sts for 5 cm (2 in) ending with a purl row.

### Shape Top

**Row 1**: (K1, k2tog) 5 times.

**Row 2**: Purl.

**Row 3**: (K2tog) 5 times.

Complete as for first finger.

### FOURTH FINGER

With RS facing, rejoin grey yarn and K2 sts from base of third finger, K to end. Cont in st st on these 16 sts for 4.5 cm (1¾ in) ending with a purl row. Shape top and finish as for third finger. Darn in all ends from chart. Leave the ribbed band open at this point, as crochet band will be worked first.

## CROCHET BORDER

With RS facing and using contrast colour, using 3 mm crochet hook, work a row of dc into cast-on edge of ribbed cuff. Turn.

**Next row**: 3ch, dc into next dc* 3ch, s s into first of 3ch, dc into next dc, rep from * to end of row. Sl st in last dc to finish off. Darn in ends. Sew up ribbed cuff and close crochet border. Fold ribbed cuff in half. Press gloves.

# LEFT-HAND GLOVE

Work as for right-hand glove reversing directions; first patt row will read K25 grey, patt 29 from chart.

### COMMENCE THUMB GUSSET

K21 grey, inc into each of next 2 sts, K2, patt 29 from chart. Work 3 rows without further shaping.

**Next row**: K21 grey, inc into next st, K2, inc into next st, K2, patt 29 from chart. Cont in this manner, inc 2 sts in thumb gusset in every fourth row until 7 incs have been worked (68 sts). (Note, increase the number of knit sts by 2 on each increase row. By the final inc row there will be 12 K sts between increases in thumb gusset.

### COMMENCE THUMB

K37 grey, turn, cast on 2 sts.

**Next row**: P18, turn, cast on 2 sts. Cont in st st. Complete as for right thumb.

Cont exactly as for right-hand glove keeping the first 25 sts in grey and the 29 patt from chart at the end of the work until chart has been complete.

# Caramel Beret

Little flowers, knitted in a mixture of Rowan Felted Tweed and Kidsilk Haze decorate this pretty and practical hat. This is a simple project that knits up quickly into a stylish beret, just perfect for those crisp autumn days.

### Size
Circumference: 56 cm (22 in)

### Tension
22–24 stitches and 30–32 rows to 10 cm (4 in) square measured over st st felted tweed. using 4 mm needles

### Materials
1 x 50 g (2 oz) ball of Rowan Felted Tweed, ginger

1 x 25 g (1 oz) ball Rowan Kidsilk Haze, orange

Pair of 4 mm (US 6) knitting needles

Pair of 3 mm (US 2/3) knitting needles

3 mm (2½) crochet hook

Wool needle, for sewing up

**Note**: Kidsilk Haze and Felted Tweed are knitted together for the ribbed band, and the crown decreases. The 24-row centre panel is worked in Felted Tweed only.

# BERET

Using 3 mm knitting needles and one strand of each yarn held together, cast on 121 sts.

**Row 1**: K2, *K1, P1 rep from * to end.

**Row 2**: K1, *P1, K1 rep from * to end.

Rep these 2 rows another three times and then first row once.

**Row 10**: Rib 1, *inc in next st, rib 1, inc in next st, rib 2, rep from * to end (169 sts).

Change to 4 mm knitting needles.

Break off Kidsilk Haze.

Work 24 rows st st, beg with a knit row.

### Shape Crown

**Row 1**: Join in Kidsilk Haze and K13, *sl 1, k2tog, psso, K25, rep from * ending last rep with K13, instead of K25 (157 sts).

Work 3 rows st st.

**Row 5**: K12, *sl 1, k2tog, K23, rep from * ending last rep with K12 instead of K23 (145 sts).

Work 3 rows st st.

**Row 9**: K11, *sl 1, k2tog, K21, rep from * ending last rep with K11 instead of K21 (133 sts).

Work 3 rows st st

**Row 13**: K10, *sl 1, k2tog, K20, rep from * ending last rep with K10 instead of K20 (121 sts).

Work 3 rows st st.

Cont dec in this manner on each fourth row until 97 sts rem, then on foll alt rows until 13 sts rem.

Break off yarn, thread through rem sts pull up tightly and fasten off.

## To Make Up

Press lightly under a damp cloth, if necessary. With right sides together join centre back seam using back stitch. Sew in any loose ends. Turn right side out.

## Flowers
## Make 3

Using 3 mm crochet hook and orange Kidsilk Haze make a slip ring, (see techniques).

**Round 1**: 2 ch, 9 dc, into the slip ring and then pull the loose end to close the ring, join with a ss in top ch of second ch.

**Round 2**: (petals) 1 ch *(1 dtr, 2 tr tr, 1 dtr) in next dc, ss in next dc, repeat from * 3 times more, (1 dtr, 2 tr tr, 1 dtr) in next dc, ss in 1ch (5 petals). Fasten off.

Sew in ends.

Sew the three flowers 5 cm (2 in) above the ribbed band and 13 cm (5 in) from centre back seam.

# Floral Brooch

*Simple to make, this attractive floral brooch is made with knitted and felted yarn, which is then embroidered. You could make this from an old thick wool jumper or use vintage fabric gleaned from a thrift store. The decoration is simple to do, so it's a great project to make if you are short of time.*

## Size
14 x 15 cm (5½ x 6 in)

## Materials
1 x 50 g (2 oz) ball of Wash+Filz-It! dark grey felting yarn
Pair of 5 mm (US 8) knitting needles
1 skein stranded embroidery cotton, red
Small amount of red merino wool for needle felting
Needle felting needle
Brooch back, 3 cm (1¼ in) long
Embroidery needle
Sewing threads, grey and red
Sewing needle
Thick foam

## BROOCH CENTRE

Take a small piece of red merino needle-felting wool, the size of a small walnut, and roll it between your palms into a tight ball. Put the ball on a piece of thick foam so that you don't stab yourself. Take the felting needle and push it in to the ball at intervals all over so that the ball becomes firm. The ball will become smaller so you may need to re-shape and add a few extra layers until it is a bit larger than a cherry, and firm all over. Set aside.

## PETALS

**1** Knit and felt the dark grey yarn according to the instructions on the yarn label.

**2** Felt the fabric according to the manufacturer's instructions. Allow to dry. Cut out five petals from the grey felted fabric.

**3** With three strands of red embroidery cotton, work a row of chain stitch 0.5 cm (¼ in) in from the edge of each petal.

**4** Using three strands of red embroidery cotton and stem stitch, work three leaf veins, starting at the centre bottom of the petal. The two leaf veins on the outside will be longer than the middle one.

**5** Take a very small amount of the red merino needle felting yarn and needle felt an oval shape in the lower section of each petal.

**6** Cut a circle for the back of flower. Using three strands of red embroidery cotton, work blanket stitch all around the edge. Using grey thread, stitch the brooch back firmly on to the centre of this piece.

### To Make Up

**1** Place the back of the flower circle on a flat surface and put the first two petals of the flower in place on top. Stitch in place. Leave a gap for the red centre piece.

**2** Place two lower petals so that the points of the petals face each other. Stitch in place. Position the top petal. It will overlap the two side petals. Stitch in place using grey thread. Take a length of red thread and the red felted ball and stitch firmly in the centre of the flower.

# Rose and Daisy Felted Pin Cushion

This large pin cushion is made of fabric that has been knitted and then felted in a washing machine. It is embroidered and beaded before being sewn together and then the crocheted flowers and knitted leaves are attached to the top.

### Size
12 cm (4¾ in) high, 12 cm (4¾ in) diameter

### Materials
2 x 50 g (2 oz) ball of Wash+Filz-It! cream felting yarn
Pair of 5 mm (US ) knitting needles
Small amount of 4-ply in bright green and three shades of pink
3 mm (US 2/3) crochet hook
2 x 2.25 mm (US 1) double-pointed knitting needles

Stranded embroidery cotton in light pink, dark pink, sage green, cream
42 x 8 mm (⅛ in) pearl beads, pale pink
Small beads, mid-green and pink
5 x 1 cm (⅜ in) crystal beads, pale pink
Sewing needle
Beading needle
Matching thread
Polyester fibre filling
Plastic pellets
Card (card stock) circle (slight smaller diameter than base)
Erasable marking pen

1 Using 5 mm (¼ in) knitting needles and cream felting yarn, cast on 35 sts. Work 2 rows garter st. Continue in stocking st until both balls have been used. Cast off.

2 Felt the piece according to the manufacturer's instruction, then allow to dry. From the felted fabric, cut one piece 29.5 x 6.5 cm (11½ x 2½ in). Cut one circle for the base, 9 cm (3½ in) diameter.

3 To finish the edges of the felted pieces whip stitch by hand using cream.

# EMBROIDERY

1 There are 8 flowers around the side of the pin cushion. Start by marking the centre position of each so that they are evenly spaced along the side and 3 cm (1¼ in) from the top edge of the work. The centre of each flower is a bullion knot made of 7 wraps curved into a circle. Alternate the colours of the flower centres. Secure the circle with a stitch to catch it down so it sits neatly.

2 The surrounding petals are made of bullion knots consisting of 9–11 wraps. To work the petals, using three strands of embroidery cotton and light pink, work nine petals evenly spaced around each flower centre.

3 The stem and leaves are worked from stem stitch. Work a 2 cm (¾ in) stem, curving it slightly to the left using three strands of sage green embroidery cotton. From each side of the bottom of the stem work two stem stitch leaves each 1 cm (³/₈ in) long.

4 Take the beading needle and a length of sewing thread and stitch the small pink beads randomly around the flowers all along the felted fabric. You don't need to use too many as there will be the pink pearl beads along the bottom and the green beads along the top.

5 Sew the pearl pink beads along the bottom edge, evenly spaced.

6 Sew the mid-green beads 5 cm (2 in) below the top edge of the side.

## To Make Up

1 With right sides together, and allowing a 5 mm (¼ in) seam, place the short edges of the side piece together and stitch in place. Turn right side out.

2 Fit one circular base to the tubular side piece. Pin in place. Using three strands of pale pink embroidery cotton and blanket stitch, sew into position.

**3** Place the circular cardboard disc in the base, then three-quarters fill the pin cushion with the plastic pellets. Carefully fill the remainder of the pin cushion with fibre filling.

**4** Attach the top of the pin cushion to the sides using three strands of dark pink embroidery cotton and blanket stitch. Keep stuffing the pin cushion as you go so that you achieve a firm, rounded dome.

## LEAVES
### Make 4

Using 2.25 mm knitting needles and 4-ply bright green, cast on 3 sts, work an I-cord for 1.5 cm (½ in).

**Row 1**: (RS) Knit.
**Row 2 and all even rows**: Knit.
**Row 3**: K1, m1, K1, m1, K1.
**Row 5**: K2, m1, K1, m1, K2.
**Row 7**: K3 m1, K1, m1, K3.

**Row 9**: K4, m1, K1, m1, K4.

**Row 11**: K5, m1, K1, m1, K5.

**Row 13 and 15**: Knit.

**Row 17**: K5, sl 2, K1, psso, K5.

**Row 19**: K4, sl 2, K1, psso, K4.

**Row 21**: K3, sl 2, K1, psso, K3.

**Row 23**: K2, sl 2, K1, psso, K2.

**Row 25**: K1, sl 2, K1, psso, K1 (3 sts).

**Row 27**: K1, sl 2, psso, fasten off.

Sew the leaves evenly spaced around the top of the pin cushion with the stems facing in towards the centre. There will be a flower in between each leaf and one in the centre.

## FLOWERS 1

### Make 5

Use a combination of pale pink, dark pink and bright pink for the flowers. Using 3 mm crochet hook and dark pink, make 4 ch, join with a ss, into a ring.

**Round 1**: (RS) 2ch, 9 dc in ring with dark pink, ss to top of 2 ch (10 sts).

**Round 2**: Using contrast pink, 5ch, 1 tr tr in each of next 9 dc, ss to top of 5ch. Fasten off. Darn in end and form into a neat circle.

## FLOWERS 2

Using 3 mm crochet hook and pink 4-ply, make a slip ring.

**Round 1**: (RS) 3ch, 15 tr into ring, pull end of yarn to close the ring, ss in top ch of 3ch (16 sts).

**Round 2**: 4ch, (ss in the front strand on next tr, 3ch) 15 times, ss in first of 4ch. Fasten off invisibly.

**Round 3**: Working behind the second round, 6 ch, working in the back strand of each tr (ss in next tr, 5ch) 15 times, ss in first of 6ch. Fasten off invisibly.

Using a beading needle and sewing thread attach a pale pink crystal bead to the centre of each flower and then sew flowers firmly to the top of the pin cushion. The three flowers will go across the top in a row and the two contrasting flowers each side interspersed with the leaves.

# Beaded Birdy Brooch

This little jewelled bird is made from a piece of needle-felted fabric, which is the heavily beaded and embroidered in gold thread. It makes a sparkling adornment for a winter coat or hat, or just for fun.

### Size
7 x 9 cm (2¾ x 3½ in)

### Materials
Foam block
Needle-felting needle
Merino needle-felting yarn in a
    mixture of reds and oranges
Beading needle
Sewing needle
Gold embroidery thread
    (Marlitt)
Matching thread
Gold jewellery wire (for legs
    and tail)
Small glass beads, red, gold

1 x 4 mm (⅛ in) black bead, for
    eye
1 x 4 mm (⅛ in) red bead, for
    tail
Brooch back, 3 cm (1¼ in)
3 x 6 mm (¼ in) Swarovski red
    crystal beads, for tail, wing
    and beak
2 x 4 mm (⅛ in) oblong red
    glass beads, for feet
10 cm (⅜ in) square red wool
    felt, for backing
Jewellery pliers

# NEEDLE FELTING

**1** Make one 12 cm (4¾ in) square of needle-felted orange and red fabric using lengths of red and orange merino wool. Arrange the wool in layers on the foam block, then stab the needle-felting needle in and out quickly and firmly. The fabric will begins to adhere and take on a dense texture. Keep adding more layers, a little at a time and stabbing with your needle until your fabric is even and firm and there are no transparent parts. It needs to be the texture of commercial felt.

**2** Cut one bird and wing from the needle-felted fabric. Cut the same from red wool felt for the backing.

**3** Using 1 strand of gold Marlitt embroidery thread, sew a line of chain stitches 5 mm (¼ in) from the edge of the needle-felted bird and wing. Marlitt thread tangles and frays quite easily so use short lengths.

**4** Using red thread, sew a row of red glass beads around the inside edge of the gold chain stitch on the bird.

**5** Stitch the Swarovski crystals to the centre of the wing inside the chain stitch. Sew the wing to the bird, aligning it with the centre back.

**6** Stitch the 4 mm (⅛ in) black bead in position for the eye.

**7** To make the legs, cut a piece of jewellery wire 5 cm (2 in) long for each. Thread a small red glass bead on one end and then fold the end of the wire over tightly to secure using pliers, if needed. Place the small red oblong bead on the wire for the foot and then continue to alternate red and gold beads along the length of the wire until you almost reach the end. Place the second oblong bead, then top with a red bead for the foot, bend back the remaining end of wire to secure. Fold the leg section in half and set aside.

**8** To make the tail, cut a length of jewellery wire 3 cm (1¼ in) long and attach a red glass bead in the same manner as for the feet. Next add the 4 mm (⅛ in) red bead and then the Swarovski crystal. Bend the remaining length of wire double and wrap matching thread tightly around it to secure. Set aside.

**9** Stitch the brooch back in place using polyester thread, positioning it 1.5 cm (½ in) below the top of the head on the red wool felt backing.

**10** Place the front and back of the bird together. Sandwich the legs between the two. Sandwich the tail in place in the same way. Hold in place with a pin.

**11** Fasten a length of thread securely to the tail, place a gold bead, a red bead and then another red bead on the needle and bring beads over to cover the top edge of the work. Continue in this manner creating a beaded edge (3 beads wide all the way around the bird) until you come to the beak, diagonally below the eye. Stitch the remaining Swarovski crystal in place and then continue with the beaded edge all the way around the bird. Ensure that you pull your cotton firmly so that the beading sits as evenly as possible.

**12** Sew 4 red glass beads along diagonal edge of wing to highlight.

# Felted Tea Cosy

This is a tea cosy for a 2–3 cup teapot and fits right over the teapot. It is designed to resemble a miniature circus tent and is made of knitted and felted fabric, embellished with felted ball, flowers and embroidery.

### Size
To fit a 2–3-cup teapot
Height: 20 cm (8 in)

### Materials
30 x 2 cm (¾ in) diameter felt balls in red, orange, yellow and brown

4 large felt daisies, 2 red, 2 orange

2 x 50 g (2 oz) ball of Wash+Filz-It! red felting yarn

2 x 50 g (2 oz) ball of Wash+Filz-It! orange felting yarn

Pair of 5 mm (US 8) knitting needles

Merino needle felting yarn in a mixture of reds and pinks, for felting ball on top of tea cosy

Needle-felting needle

Foam mat

Sewing thread

Sewing needle

Stranded embroidery cottons, red and orange

# TEA COSY

**1** Knit and felt the orange and then the red yarn, according to the instructions on the yarn label.

**2** Felt the fabric according to the manufacturer's instructions. Allow to dry. Using the large triangular template, cut 3 red and 3 orange pieces from the felted fabrics.

**3** With right sides together and using red embroidery cotton and blanket stitch, sew the panels together, alternating the colours. Make sure you keep the stitches very close together to ensure a firm seam line. Once completed, turn the other way out.

**4** Stitch a line of orange chain stitch 5 mm (¼ in) from the bottom edge and then whip this chain stitch with red.

**5** Sew the 30 felted balls above the chain stitch, five on each panel.

**6** Sew the felt daisies to the top of the tea cosy, alternating the red and orange.

**7** Roll the merino needle-felting wool into a ball the size of a large walnut. Place on the foam mat, and needle felt into a firm ball, adding more yarn, if necessary. Keep rolling the ball between your palms so you achieve a nice round shape. Stitch to the top of the cosy, sewing right through the ball and the felted layers of the tea cosy.

# Antique Rose Hot Water Bottle Cover

There's nothing better than snuggling up in your favourite armchair in winter with a good book and a comforting 'hottie'. This hot water bottle is knitted in fine mohair yarn making it a perfect luxury gift.

## Size

To fit a standard hot water bottle, 36 x 23 cm (14 x 9 in)

## Materials

1 x 50 g (2 oz) ball Noro Silk Garden Lite

1 x 50 g (2 oz) ball DK (8-ply) mohair

Pair of 4 mm (US 6) knitting needles

2 x 2.75 mm (US 2) double-pointed knitting needles

Wool needle, for sewing up

# HOT WATER BOTTLE COVER

## Make 2

Using 4 mm knitting needles and Noro Silk Garden Lite, cast on 56 sts for neck cuff.

Work in K2, P2 rib for 5 cm (2 in).

**Next row**: K1, *yfwd, K2tog, rep from * to last st, K1.

Work another 5 cm (2 in) K2, P2 rib in Noro Silk Garden Lite.

Break of yarn and join in DK (8-ply) mohair.

Work in garter st (every row knit) for 23 cm (9 in).

**Next row**: Sl l, k2tog, psso, knit to last 3 sts, K3tog.

Rep this row until 16 sts rem.

Cast off.

## I-CORD TIE

Using 2 x 2.75 mm double-pointed knitting needles and mohair, cast on 3 sts.

**Row 1**: *K3, slide sts to the other end of needle, pull yarn firmly behind sts, rep from * until cord is 50 cm (20 in) long. Sl 1, k2tog, psso, fasten off. Darn in all thread ends.

## To Make Up

Place the hot water bottle front and back right sides together and stitch side and bottom seams using matching thread and back stitch. Darn in all the loose ends. Turn right side out. Place hot water bottle in hot water bottle cover. Thread the I-cord through the eyelet holes and tie in a bow.

# Autumn Leaf Brooch

Add this lovely autumn leaf brooch to your winter coat or hat and it will certainly brighten your day. It is made from knitted, felted fabric and is lightly needle-felted over the top before being embroidered and beaded. It will become a little wearable treasure.

## Size
11 x 10 cm (4½ x 4 in)

## Materials
1 x 50 g (2 oz) ball of Wash+Filz-It! orange felting yarn

Pair of 5 mm (US 8 ) knitting needles

15 x 15 cm (6 x 6 in) wool felt, sienna, for backing

Beading needle

Brooch back, 3 cm (1¼ in) long

Small amount merino needle-felting yarn in red, cream, brown and orange

Small amount 4-ply yarn for acorn, beige and dark brown

Pair of 2.25 mm (US 1) double-pointed knitting needles

Small amount of polyester fibre filling, for stuffing acorn

Wool needle

Stranded embroidery cotton in mauve, green, brown, gold, dark brown, beige

Small glass beads for base of acorn

Dark brown sewing thread

Needle-felting needle

Chalk pencil

## ACORN
### Make 2

Using 2.25 mm double-pointed knitting needles
and dark brown 4-ply, cast on 6 sts.

**Row 1**: (RS) Inc in each st (12 sts).

**Row 2**: Inc in each st (24 sts).

**Row 3**: *K1, P1, rep from * to end.

**Row 4**: *P1, K1, rep from * to end.

Rep rows 3 and 4 twice more.

**Row 9**: *P1, p2tog, rep from * to end.

Break off dark brown and join in beige.

Commencing with a purl row, work 7 rows st st.

**Row 17**: *K2tog, K2, rep from * to end.

**Row 18**: Purl.

**Row 19**: *K2tog, K1, rep from * to end.

**Row 20**: P2tog 4 times. Break off yarn, thread
through rem 4 sts, pull up tightly and fasten off.

## STEM
### Make 2

Using dark brown, cast on 10 sts. Cast off.
Attach stem to cast-on edge of acorn. Join seam
with ladder stitch on the right side and fill firmly
with polyester fibre filling as you sew the seam.

With dark brown thread and a beading
needle, sew the brown glass beads to the base
of the acorn so that they completely cover the
base, except for the last row before the beige
starts. Tie off very firmly, ensuring that the beads
sit snugly. Set aside.

## AUTUMN LEAF

**1** Knit and felt the orange yarn according to the
instructions on the yarn label.

**2** Felt the fabric according to the manufacturer's
instructions. Allow to dry. Using the template cut
out 1 leaf from the felted orange fabric and 1
leaf for backing from the sienna wool felt.
Set aside.

**3** Needle felt the orange felted leaf very lightly
all over using a mixture of the red, orange,
brown and beige merino felting wool. Aim for a
hint of colour rather than layers. Work in small
sections to create a swirling pattern rather than
straight lines. Embroidery will be worked over
the top.

## EMBROIDERY

All embroidery is worked using 3 strands except
where otherwise stated.

**1** Work a row of whipped chain stitch around
the outside of the leaf.

**2** Create the centre lines and the little veins
using stem stitch and 2 strands of mauve and
1 strand of gold in the needle at the same time.

**3** The dark brown swirls in the rounded outer
parts of the leaf are worked in stem stitch.

**4** The loops down the sides of the leaf veins are worked in green, using 17-wrap bullion knots. There are 3 bullion knots under each shoot of the central leaf vein, and 2 bullion knots at the top of the leaf.

## STEM

Cut a 3 x 1 cm (1¼ x ³⁄₈ in) piece of brown felt. Fold along long edge into three leaving top 5 mm (¼ in) flat (this will join into the leaf base). Stitch folded edge closed. Cover the rolled stem piece with beads as for base of acorn.

### ATTACH ACORN

Sew the acorn to the lower right corner of the leaf stitching through all layers so that the acorn is securely attached.

Centre the brooch back on the sienna felt piece. Sew front and back of leaf together using matching thread and very small stitches. When you get to the base of the leaf, sandwich the stem into position between the front and the back, stitching through the 5 mm (¼ in) un-beaded section. Continue stitching all the way around.

# Retro Tea Cosy

This six-cup tea cosy in clashing mauves, oranges and pinks will keep your tea hot. It is knitted in two halves, which are stitched together. On top sits a handful of decorative bells.

**Size**
To fit: 6-cup teapot

**Materials**
1 x 50 g (2 oz) ball in DK (8-ply), pink
2 x 50 g (2 oz) balls in DK (8-ply), orange (O)
2 x 50 g (2 oz) balls in DK (8-ply), mauve (M)
Small amounts of DK (8-ply) for embellishments in variegated pink, pale orange, medium pink and pale pink

Pair of 4 mm (US 6) knitting needles
2 x 2.75 mm (US 2) double-pointed knitting needles
Wool needle
Sewing needle
Polyester fibre filling

# TEA COSY

The pleated fabric is created by pulling the yarn not in use tightly on the wrong side. It is important to do this on each row. Carry the yarn on the back of the work and right across to the ends. It may seem a little slow to begin with but you will develop a rhythm.

## Make 2

Using 4 mm knitting needles and pink DK (8-ply), cast on 98 sts. Work 8 rows garter st. Cut off pink and join in orange and mauve.

**Row 9**: K1m, K6o, *K7m, K7o, rep from * to last 7 sts, K6m, K1o. As you knit pull the yarn not in use very firmly behind, to draw up the pleats.

**Row 10**: K1o, K6m, *K7o, K6m, rep from * to last 7 sts, K6o, K1m. Keep yarn to the front in this row and continue to pull the yarn not in use tightly so that pleats remain firm.

These 2 rows form patt. Continue in patt until 48 rows have been worked.

### Shaping

**Row 1**: (RS) K2togm, K3o, k2togo, *k2togm, K3m, K2togo, K3o, k2togo, rep from * to last 7 sts, k2togm, K3m, K2togo.

**Row 2**: K1o, K4m, *K5o, K5m, rep from * to last 5 sts, K4o, K1m.

**Row 3**: K2togm, K1o, K2togo, * k2togm, K1m, k2togm, K2togo, K1o, k2togo rep from * to last 5 sts, k2togm, K1m, K2togo.

**Row 4**: K1o, K2m, *K3o, K3m, rep from * to last 3 sts, K2o, K1m.

**Row 5**: K2togm, K1o, *k2togo, K1m, k2togo, K1o, rep from * to last 3 sts, k2togm, k1o.

**Row 6**: K1o, K1m, *K2o, K2m, rep from * to last 2 sts, K1o, K1m.

**Row 7**: (K2togm) twice, *k2togo, k2togm, rep from * to last 4 sts, (k2togo) twice.

Break off yarn, thread through rem sts, pull up tightly and fasten off.

Darn in any loose ends. With right sides together, stitch from the centre top down each side for 5 cm (2 in). Be sure to end off very firmly. Join sides together at the bottom edge, stitching up each side for 3–4 cm (1¼–1½ in). Turn right side out.

## BELLS

Make 4 bells; 1 bright orange, 1 variegated pink, 1 medium pink and 1 pale orange.

Using 2.75 mm knitting needles and DK (8-ply), cast on 13 sts.

**Row 1**: K1, inc into every st to end (25 sts).

**Row 2**: Beg with a purl row, st st 10 rows. (This becomes the lining section.)

**Row 3**: K1, (yrn, k2tog) to end.

Beg with a knit row work 12 rows st st.

**Next row**: K1, (k2tog, K1) to end (17 sts).

**Next row**: Purl.

**Next row**: K1, (k2tog) to end (9 sts).

Break of yarn, thread through rem sts, pull up tightly and fasten off.

Oversew the row ends together and turn right side out. Tuck the lining section inside the bell.

## I-CORDS

Make 4 I-cords for attaching the bells, 1 x 11 cm (4¼ in) medium pink, 1 x 9 cm (3½ in) pale pink, 1 x 7 cm (2¾ in) pale orange, 1 x 8 cm (3 in) medium pink.

Using 2.75 mm double-pointed knitting needles and DK (8-ply) in desired shade, cast on 3 sts. *K3, slide sts to end of needle, pull yarn firmly behind sts, do not turn work, rep from * until cord is desired length.
Sl 1, k2tog, psso, fasten off.

Stitch one end of the I-cord to the top of the bell and the other end to the top of the tea cosy. The pale orange I-cord stitches to the medium pink bell. The medium pink I-cord stitches to the bright orange bell. The medium pink I-cord stitches to the pale orange bell and the pale pink I-cord stitches to the variegated pink bell.

## KNITTED BALLS

Make 4 knitted balls, 1 bright orange, 1 pale orange, 1 medium pink and 1 pale pink.

Using 2.75 mm knitting needles and DK (8-ply) in desired shade, cast on 12 sts.
**Row 1**: Knit

**Row 2**: P10, wrap.
**Row 3**: K8, wrap.
**Row 4**: P6, wrap.
**Row 5**: K4, wrap.
**Row 6**: Purl.
Rep these 6 rows another 4 times. Cast off.
With right sides together, sew side seam halfway. Turn right side out and stuff firmly. Sew the remainder of the seam and then run a gathering thread around the cast-on edge. Pull up firmly and fasten off. Do the same with the other end. Make sure you have sufficient filling and have made a firm round ball.
Sew the balls to the top of the tea cosy.

# Nightdress Case

Keep delicate fabrics safe in this pretty nightdress case. Decorate the flap with fun daisies for an over-the-top feminine look for a young girl, or keep it plain and restrained. Make the case in colours that complement your soft furnishing fabrics.

**Measurements**
30 x 30 cm (12 x 12 in)

**Materials**
2 x 50 g (2 oz) balls, DK (8-ply) cotton, dark purple
Oddments of 4-ply for the daisies, pale pink, bright pink, purple, mauve
Pair of 4 mm (US 6) knitting needles
3 mm (US 11) crochet hook
2 x 2.75 mm (US 2) double-pointed knitting needles
Wool needle, for sewing up
Lining fabric, 35 x 75 cm (14 x 30 in)
Matching thread
Sewing needle
Pins

## DAISIES

Each daisy is made with 2 colours. Use the first colour for the first three rounds and the second colour for rounds four and five. Make eight daisies in a mixture of shades.

Using 3 mm crochet hook and first colour, make 2ch.

**Round 1**: 9 dc into second ch from hook, join with a ss into first dc.

**Round 2**: 4ch, ss into front loop of first dc, (4ch, ss into front of loop of next dc) 8 times, ss into first ss.

**Round 3**: 1ch, 2 dc into back of loop of first dc, 2 dc into back of loop of each of next 8 dc, ss into first dc.

**Round 4**: Break off first colour and join in second colour, 6 ch, sl st into front of loop of first dc, (6ch, ss into front of loop of next dc) 17 times, ss into first ss.

**Round 5**: 8ch, ss, into back of loop of first dc, (8ch, ss into back of loop of next dc) 17 times. Ss into first ss. Fasten off.

# NIGHTDRESS CASE

Using 4 mm knitting needles and DK (8-ply) cotton, cast on 64 sts.
Work 2 rows garter st.
Commence diamond pattern. Work in pattern for 70 cm (27½ in) ending with an eighth pattern row.

### DIAMOND PATTERN (8-ROW REPEAT)

**Row 1**: (RS) *P1, K7, rep from * to end.
**Rows 2 and 8**: *K1, P5, K1, P1, rep from * to end.
**Rows 3 and 7**: *K2, P1, K3, P1, K1, rep from * to end.
**Rows 4 and 6**: *P2, K1, P1, K1, P3, rep from * to end.
**Row 5**: *K4, P1, K3, rep from * to end.
These 8 rows form the patt.
Work 2 rows garter st.
Cast off.

## To Make Up

**1** Darn in all loose ends. Press lightly and block to ensure an even shape.

**2** Cut the lining fabric to the dimensions of the nightdress case adding a 1.5 cm (¾ in) seam allowance to each side.

**3** Fold the seam allowance under and press. Pin the lining in place, wrong sides together. Pin the corners first, to reduce puckering. Sew in place with a blind hem. Make sure your stitches are very close together.

**4** Fold up the first 25 cm (10 in) of the bag, lining sides together and stitch side seams using mattress stitch.

**5** Pin the daisies to the top flap in two rows, staggering them so they are slightly offset. Use matching thread to sew them in place.

## I-cord Ties
### Make 4
Using 2 x 2.75 mm knitting needles and DK (8-ply) cotton, cast on 3 sts.

**Row 1**: *K3, slide sts to the other end of needle, pull yarn firmly behind sts, rep from * until cord is 15 cm (6 in) long.

Sl 1, k2tog, psso, fasten off.
Sew two I-cords 5 cm (2 in) from the edge of the flap and the remaining two I-cords, 5 cm (2 in) in from the edge on main case. Tie cords in a bow.

# Crocheted Cardigan Collar

This pretty crocheted and beaded collar can be added to a purchased or hand-knitted cardigan. Made in white crochet cotton, it has Swarovski crystal beads stitched into the design to give it weight and an opulent effect.

## Materials

Cardigan or jumper with round
   neck
1 x 50 g (2 oz) ball Grignasco
   Cotton 5, crochet cotton
1.75 mm (USA 4 ) crochet hook
6 mm (¼ in) pale pink
   Swarovski crystal beads
   (I used 41)
Matching thread
Sewing needle
Wool needle, for darning
   in ends
Beading needle

# CROCHET COLLAR

Using 1.75 mm crochet hook and crochet cotton, make a foundation ch long enough to go around the collar of the cardigan. This needs to be a multiple of 4.

**Row 1**: 1 dc, into second ch from hook, 1 dc into each ch to end.

**Row 2**: 1ch, 1 dc, into first 1 dc, *4ch, miss 1 dc, 1 dc into next ch, rep from * to end.

**Row 3**: 5ch, (counts as 1 tr and 2ch), 1 dc into first 4ch sp, *4ch 1 dc into next 4ch sp; rep from * to end 2ch, 1 tr into last dc.

**Row 4**: 1ch, 1 dc, into tr, 6ch, *1 dc into next 4ch sp, 6ch; rep from * end, 1 dc into third of 5ch.

**Row 5**: 1ch, 1 dc, into tr, 6ch, *1 dc into next 6ch sp, 6ch; rep from * end, 1 dc into third of 5ch.

**Row 6**: 6ch, (counts as 1 tr and 3ch), 1 dc into first 6ch sp,* 9ch, 1 dc into sixth ch from hook, 6ch, 1dc into same ch, 5ch, 1dc into same ch, 3ch 1 dc into next 6ch sp, rep from * to end, 3ch, 1 tr into last dc.

Fasten off.

## To Make Up

Sew in all ends. Using warm iron and damp cloth, press crocheted piece.

Using matching thread and sewing needle, sew crocheted collar to collar of cardigan with wrong sides together.

Using a beading needle and thread sew a Swarovski crystal bead to the point of alternate picot edge points. Secure each bead firmly.

# Face Cloth and Soap Bag

Knitted cotton washcloths are great projects for beginning knitters and are very popular with mums who want to use pure cotton on their baby's soft skin. This washcloth and soap bag set is quickly knitted and would make an ideal gift for a baby shower.

## Size

*Washcloth*
22 x 22 cm (8½ x 8½ in)

*Soap Bag*
17 x 13 cm (6½ x 5 in)

## Materials

1 x 50 g (2 oz) ball Sirdar DK (8-ply) Cotton, pink
Pair of 4.5 mm (US 7) knitting needles
1 m (40 in) of 5 mm (¼ in)-wide pink gingham ribbon
3 x 1.5 cm (½ in) diameter pink buttons (decorative use only, for soap bag)
Wool needle, for sewing up
Matching thread
Sewing needle

# FACE CLOTH

Using 4.5 mm knitting needles and DK (8-ply)
cotton, cast on 45 sts.

Work 8 rows garter st.

**Row 1**: K4, P1, *sl 1 purlwise, P1, rep from * to
last 5 sts, P1, K4.

**Row 2**: K4, purl to last 4 sts, K4.

**Row 3**: K4, P2, * sl 1 purlwise, P1, rep from * to
last 6 sts, P2, K4.

**Row 4**: K4, purl to last 4 sts, K4.

These 4 rows form patt. Work in patt until work
measures 18 cm (7 in) ending with a row 3. Work
8 rows garter st. Cast off.

## To Make Up

Darn in all ends. Take a 10 cm (4 in) length of
pink gingham ribbon, form into a bow and using
matching thread stitch firmly into one corner of
the washcloth.

# SOAP BAG

Using 4.5 mm knitting needles, cast on 59 sts.
Work 8 rows garter st as for face cloth.

**Eyelet row**: K1, *yfwd, k2tog, rep from * to last
st, K1.

**Next row**: Knit.

Work 4-row pattern as for face cloth until cloth
measures 17 cm (6¾ in) ending on a row 4.
Cast off.

## To Make Up

Fold soap bag in half, right sides together, and
using a back stitch, sew side and bottom edges.
Turn right side out. Thread ribbon through the
eyelet holes. Sew the buttons to the front of the
soap bag, using matching thread and sewing
needle. Stitch the first 5 cm (2 in) from the top
edge and the rest 1.5 cm (½ in) apart. Tie ribbon
in a bow.

# Dahlia Headband

Little girls always love headbands and hair slides. These pretty hairbands are made in pure cotton in toning shades of pretty pink and will be a hit with any little budding fairy or princess.

## Materials

Plain headband

1 x 50 g (2 oz) ball 4-ply cotton, pale pink

1 x 50 g (2 oz) ball 4-ply cotton, bright pink

1 x 50 g (2 oz) ball 4-ply cotton, pale green

1 x 50 g (2 oz) ball 4-ply cotton, bright green

1 m (40 in) x 2 cm (¾ in wide) ribbon, pale pink

Sewing thread, pink

Sewing needle

Double-sided tape

2 x 2.25 mm (US 1) double-pointed knitting needles

3 mm (US 11) crochet hook

## HEADBAND

Place a small piece of double-sided tape at each end of the inside of the headband.

Fold the raw edge of the ribbon edge in, then wrap the ribbon around the headband in a diagonal manner. Ensure that it is firm and flat, then stitch in position on the inside of the headband. Fold the ribbon end to the inside so that you have a neat edge. Stitch the other end firmly so that it does not come unwrapped.

## DAHLIAS

Make 2 bright pink flowers with a pale pink centre and 1 pale pink flower with a bright pink centre. Use the first colour for the first three rounds and the second colour for rounds four and five.

Using a 3 mm crochet hook and first colour, make 2ch.

**Round 1**: 9 dc into second ch from hook, join with a ss into first dc.

**Round 2**: 4ch, ss into front loop of first dc, (4ch, ss into front of loop of next dc) 8 times, ss into first ss.

**Round 3**: 1ch, 2 dc into back of loop of first dc, 2 dc into back of loop of each of next 8 dc, ss into first dc.

**Round 4**: Break off first colour and join in second colour, 6ch, sl st into front of loop of first dc, (6ch, ss into front of loop of next dc) 17 times, ss into first ss.

**Round 5**: 8ch, ss, into back of loop of first dc, (8ch, ss into back of loop of next dc) 17 times. Ss into first ss. Fasten off.

## LEAVES

Make 4: 2 bright green and 2 pale green

Using 2.25 mm knitting needles and bright green 4-ply, cast on 3 sts. Make an I-cord for 1.5 cm (½ in).

**Row 1**: (RS) Knit.

**Row 2**: Knit.

**Row 3**: K1, m1, K1, m1, K1.

**Row 4 and all even rows**: Knit.

**Row 5**: K2, m1, K1, m1, K2.

**Row 7**: K3, m1, K1, m1, K3.

**Row 9**: K4, m1, K1, m1, K4.

**Row 11**: K5, m1, K1, m1, K5.

**Rows 13 and 15**: Knit.

**Row 17**: K5, sl 2, K1, psso, K5.

**Row 19**: K4, sl 2, K1, psso, K4.

**Row 21**: K3, sl 2, K1, psso, K3.

**Row 23**: K2, sl 2, K1, psso, K2.

**Row 25**: K1, sl 2, K1, psso, K1 (3 sts).

**Row 27**: K1, sl 2, psso, fasten off.

## To Make Up

Sew the three flowers to the top of the headband with the bright pink ones on each side of the pale pink one. Sew a bright green leaf to one side of a bright pink flower and the other bright green leaf between the bright pink and pale pink flower. Sew the pale green leaves to each side of the pale pink flowers.

*Dahlia headband* / 115

# Little Flower Hair Clip

These little crocheted and knitted flower hairslides will delight any little girl. They are quick to make and look effective. You could replace the hairslide with a brooch back, if you like.

## Materials

1 spring-loaded hair clip, 8 cm (3 in) long
Small amounts of 4-ply pure wool, pale pink, bright pink, pale green and bright green
3 mm (US 11) crochet hook
Pair of 2.75 mm (US 2) double-pointed knitting needles
Wool needle
Double-sided tape
Small piece of pink felt
Matching thread
Sewing needle

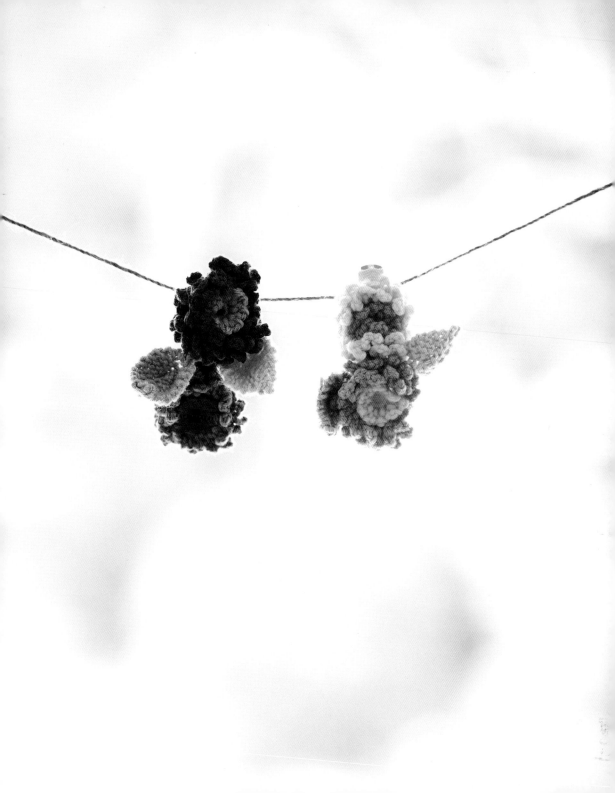

## HAIR SLIDE

Cut a piece of double-sided tape and place along the flat top of the hair slide. Do not cover up the hole at each end.

Cut a piece of felt the same length as the hair slide and stick to the double-sided tape. Secure in place with a few stitches through the holes at each end of the slide.

## FLOWERS

Make 2, 1 with a bright pink centre and pale pink outer, and 1 with the reverse colourscheme.

Using 3 mm crochet hook and first colour, make 2ch.

**Round 1**: 9 dc into second ch from hook, join with a ss into first dc.

**Round 2**: 4ch, ss into front loop of first dc, (4ch, ss into front of loop of next dc) 8 times, sl st into first ss.

**Round 3**: 1ch, 2 dc into back of loop of first dc, 2 dc into back of loop of each of next 8 dc, ss into first dc.

**Round 4**: Break off first colour and join in second colour, 6 ch, sl st into front of loop of first dc, (6ch, ss into front of loop of next dc) 17 times. Sl st into first ss.

**Round 5**: 8ch, ss into back of loop of first dc, (8ch, ss into back of loop of next dc) 17 times. Ss into first sl st. Fasten off.

Darn in any loose ends.

## LEAVES

Make 2, one in each shade of green.

Using 2.75 mm double-pointed knitting needles and 4-ply bright green, cast on 3 sts, work an I-cord for 1.5 cm (½ in) for the stem of the leaf. Continue as follows:

**Row 1**: (RS) Knit.

**Row 2**: Knit.

**Row 3**: K1, m1, K1, m1, K1.

**Row 4 and all even rows**: Knit.

**Row 5**: K2, m1, K1, m1, K2.

**Row 7**: K3, m1, K1, m1, K3.

**Row 9**: K4, m1, K1, m1, K4.

**Row 11**: K5, m1, K1, m1, K5.

**Rows 13 and 15**: Knit.

**Row 17**: K5, sl 2, K1, psso, K5.

**Row 19**: K4, sl 2, K1, psso, K4.

**Row 21**: K3, sl 2, K1, psso, K3.

**Row 23**: K2, sl 2, K1, psso, K2.

**Row 25**: K1, sl 2, K1, psso, K1 (3 sts).

**Row 27**: K1, sl 2, psso, fasten off.

Darn in all loose ends

### To Make Up

Sew the flowers to each end of the clip and stitch the leaves to each side between the flowers.

# Crocheted Heart Motif for a Vest

This simple heart shape with crocheted edging looks sweet and stylish. When used to embellish a vest it makes a cute gift for a new baby. Alternatively you could add it to a T-shirt for a larger baby or toddler.

## Materials

Cotton vest
15 x 15 cm (6 x 6 in) piece of
  fusible interfacing
Scissors
Pencil
15 x 15 cm (6 x 6 in) piece of
  floral cotton fabric
Iron and ironing board
1 x 20 g (¾ oz) ball Coats 20
  Crochet Cotton, pink
1.75 mm (US 2) crochet hook

Matching thread
Pins
Sewing needle
Sewing machine
Cardboard

**1** Put the fusible interfacing glue-side down (slightly rough side) and put the heart template on top. The template should measure 9 cm (3½ in) at its widest part by 9 cm (3½ in) at tallest part. Draw around the shape. Roughly cut out the shape.

**2** Place glue side down on the wrong side of the floral fabric and fuse in place with a hot iron. Cut out the heart exactly on the drawn line.

**3** Set the sewing machine to a very narrow zigzag and stitch all around the edge of the heart.

## CROCHET BORDER

Using 1.75 mm crochet hook and Coats 20 crochet cotton, make a length of chain, (in multiples of 3) long enough to go right around the heart, allowing a little extra for the point, plus 2 extra ch.

**Row 1**: 1 dc, into second ch from hook, 1 dc into each ch to end.

**Row 2**: 1ch, 1 dc into first dc, *5ch, miss 2 dc, 1 dc into next dc, rep from * to end.

**Row 3**: 1ch, (3 dc, 3ch, 3 dc) into each 5ch sp to end. Fasten off.

Darn in loose ends and press flat with warm iron under a damp cloth. Do not stretch.

### To Make Up

**1** Beginning at the top of the heart, pin the crocheted ribbon in place with wrong sides together. Using matching polyester thread stitch the border to the edge of the heart using small stitches.

**2** Slide a piece of cardboard inside the vest just behind the place where the motif will go. Pin the motif in place 3 cm (1¼ in) below the centre neckline. Remove the cardboard. Stitch in place.

# Little Blue Bonnet

This simple baby's hat design has a rolled brim and is made of 100 per cent angora making it a luxuriously soft gift for a baby. Omit the flower if making for a boy

### Size

To fit: New born–6 months, (6–12 months)

### Tension

32 sts and 40 rows to 10 cm (4 in) square measured over st st on 3.25 mm (US 3) needles
This is a slightly firmer tension than would often be used for this yarn.

### Materials

2 x 10 g (½ oz) balls angora by Plymouth Yarns, pale blue
Pair of 3.25 mm (US 3) knitting needles
3 mm (US 11) crochet hook
Wool needle, for sewing up

## HAT

Using 3.25 mm knitting needles and yarn, cast on 78, (89) sts.

Work in st st until work measures 10.5 (11.5) cm / 4 (4½) in from cast-on edge.

### CROWN SHAPING

**Row 1**: K1, *K2, K9, rep from * to end.

**Row 2 and all alt rows**: Purl.

**Row 3**: K1, *k2tog, K8, rep from * to end.

**Row 5**: K1, *k2tog, K7, rep from * to end.

**Row 7**: K1, *k2tog, K6, rep from * to end.

**Row 9**: K1, *k2tog, K5, rep from * to end.

**Row 11**: K1, *k2tog, K4, rep from * to end.

**Row 13**: K1, *k2tog, K3, rep from * to end.

**Row 15**: K1, *k2tog, K2, rep from * to end.

**Row 17**: K1, *k2tog, K1, rep from * to end.

**Row 19**: K1, *k2tog, rep from * to end.

Break off yarn, thread through rem sts, pull up tightly and fasten off.

### To Make Up

With right sides together and using mattress or back stitch, carefully sew back seam, reversing, the position of the stitching on the lower 3 cm (1¼ in) for rolled edge. (Because the hat has a rolled up edge you sew most of the seam right sides together, but the last little bit wrong sides together so when it rolls to the outside you won't see the seamed edge.) Darn in any loose ends.

## FLOWER

Using 3 mm crochet hook and yarn, make a slip ring.

**Round 1**: (RS) 3ch, 15 tr into ring, pull end of yarn to close the ring, ss in top ch of 3ch (16 sts).

**Round 2**: 4ch, (ss in the front strand on next tr, 3ch) 15 times, ss in first of 4ch. Fasten off invisibly.

**Round 3**: Working behind the second round, 6ch, working in the back strand of each tr (ss in next tr, 5ch) 15 times, ss in first of 6 ch. Fasten off invisibly.

Stitch the flower to the hat front, slightly to one side.

# Winter Blues Gloves

These gloves feature tiny-cabled bands, which run all the way up each finger. These are achieved by twisted stitches. The pattern features reverse stocking stitch and a striped cuff.

**Size**

To fit 15–18 cm (6–7 in) hand length

**Tension**

24 sts and 40 rows to 10 cm (4 in) square measured over reverse st st when knitted on 3 mm (US 2/3) knitting needles

**Materials**

1 x 50 g (2 oz) ball Filatura di Crosa Zarina 4 ply, dark blue

2 x 50 g (2 oz) balls Filatura di Crosa Zarina 4 ply, royal blue

Pair of 3 mm (US 2/3) knitting needles

Wool needle, for sewing up

## SPECIAL ABBREVIATIONS

**Twist A**: K into the back of the second st on the left-hand needle then K into the front of the first st and sl both sts off needle tog.

**Twist B**: K into the front of the second st on the left-hand needle and then into the front of the first st, and sl both sts off needle tog.

**Twist C**: P into the back of the second st on the left-hand needle, then into the front of the first st, and sl both sts off tog.

**Twist D**: P into the front of the second st on the left-hand needle, then into the front of the first st, and sl both sts off tog.

## RIGHT-HAND GLOVE

Using 3 mm knitting needles and royal blue 4-ply, cast on 58 sts.

**Row 1**: K2, P2 to end.

**Row 2**: P2, K2 to end. Join in dark blue yarn.

**Row 3**: K2, P2 to end, dark blue.

**Row 4**: P2, K2 to end, dark blue.

Rep these 4 rows another 5 times, alternating the colours every two rows as set.

Commence patt as follows. *Fronts of fingers and palms are worked in reverse st st.

**Row 1**: P1, (K5, P2) 4 times, P to end.

**Row 2**: K31, (P5, K2) 3 times, P5, K1.

**Row 3**: P1, *Twist A, K1, Twist B, P2, rep from * 3 times, P2, P twice into next st, P to end.

**Row 4**: K32, *Twist C, P1, Twist D, K2, rep from * ending K1, instead of K2.

**Row 5**: P1, (K5, P2) 4 times, P twice into each of the next 2 sts. P to end.

**Row 6**: K34, *P5, K2, rep from * ending K1 instead of K2.

**Row 7**: P1, *Twist A, K1, Twist B, P2, rep from * 3 times, P to end.

**Row 8**: K34, *Twist C, P1, Twist D, K2, rep from * ending K1 instead of K2.

**Row 9**: P1, (K5, P2) 4 times, P2, inc in the next st, P2, inc in the next st, P to the end.

Rep rows 6–9 inclusive 5 more times.

**\* Note**: There will be 2 extra sts in the thumb gusset after each inc row. Work next inc as follows: P2, inc in next st, P4, inc in next st, P to end) (73 sts).

Work another 3 rows patt.

### COMMENCE THUMB

With right side facing work 48 sts, turn, K17, cast on 3 sts, continue on these 20 sts for 5 cm (2 in).

### SHAPE TOP

With right side facing, *P1, P2tog, P4, P2tog, P1, rep from * once.

**Row 2**: Knit.

**Row 3**: *P1, P2tog, P2, P2tog, P1, rep from * once. Break off yarn, thread through rem sts, pull up tightly and fasten off. Carefully sew side seam.

Pick up 3 sts from the base of the thumb and purl to the end of the row. Cont in patt on all sts for another 3.5 cm (1¼ in), commencing on a

sixth patt row.

### First Finger

With right side facing, patt 38 sts, turn, patt 17 sts, turn, cast on 3 sts, cont in patt on these 20 sts for another 6 cm (2¼ in).

### Shape Top

With right side facing, P1, p2tog, P1, patt 5, p2tog, (P2, p2tog) twice, P1.

**Next row**: Work in patt.

**Next row**: P1, p2tog, K2, k2tog, K1, p2tog, P2, p2tog. Break off yarn, thread through rem sts, pull up tightly and fasten off. Carefully sew side seam.

Break off yarn, thread through rem sts, pull up tightly and fasten off. Carefully sew side seam.

### Second Finger

With right side facing, pick up 3 sts from base of first finger. P7, turn, patt 17 sts, turn, cast on 3 sts. Cont in patt on these 20 sts for 6.5 cm (2½ in). Shape top and finish as for first finger.

### Third Finger

With right side facing, pick up 3 sts from base of second finger. P7, turn, patt 17 sts, turn, cast on 3 sts. Cont in patt on these 20 sts for 6 cm (2¼ in). Shape top and finish as for first finger.

### Fourth Finger

With right side facing, pick up 3 sts from base of third finger. P to end. Cont in patt on these 17 sts for 4.5 cm (1¾ in).

### Shape Top

With right side facing, P1, patt 5, P2, (P2, p2tog)

twice.

**Next row**: Work in patt.

**Next row**: K2tog, K1, k2tog, K1, P1, p2tog, P2, p2tog. Break off yarn, thread through rem sts, pull up tightly and fasten off. Sew side seam. Sew in all ends and sew ribbed seam closed. Press carefully if needed.

# LEFT-HAND GLOVE

Using 3 mm knitting needles and royal blue 4-ply, cast on 58 sts.

**Row 1**: K2, P2 to end, royal blue.

**Row 2**: P2, K2 to end, royal blue.

**Row 3**: K2, P2 to end, dark blue.

**Row 4**: P2, K2 to end, dark blue.

Rep these 4 rows another 5 times.

Commence patt as follows. * Fronts of fingers and palms are worked in reverse st st.

**Row 1**: P31, (K5, P2) 3 times, K5, P1.

**Row 2**: K1, (P5, K2) 4 times, K to end.

**Row 3**: P25, P twice into the next st, P5, *Twist A, K1, Twist B, P2, rep from * 3 times ending P1, instead of P2.

**Row 4**: K1, *Twist C, P1, Twist D, K2, rep from * 3 times, K to end.

**Row 5**: P25, P twice into each of the next 2 sts. Patt to end.

Cont in patt inc 2 sts in thumb gusset in every fourth row as for right-hand glove until the 6 increases have been worked (73 sts).

Work another 3 rows patt.

## Left Thumb

P 42, turn, cast on 3 sts.

**Next row**: K20, turn and cont on these 20 sts.

Complete as for right thumb.

## First Finger

With right side facing, patt 38, turn, cast on 3, patt 20, cont in patt on these 20 sts. Work as for first finger of right glove. Finish as for right glove, reversing shaping.

## Second Finger

With right side facing, pick up 3 sts from base of first finger, patt 7, turn, cast on 3 sts, patt 20, cont in patt on these 20 sts and finish as for first finger.

## Third Finger

With right side facing, pick up 3 sts from base of second finger, patt 7, turn, cast on 3 sts, patt 20, cont in patt on these 20 sts and finish as for first finger.

## Fourth Finger

With right side facing, pick up 3 sts from base of third finger. Purl to end. Cont in patt on these 17 sts for 4.5 cm (1¾ in), and finish as for fourth finger of right glove, reversing shaping.

Sew in all ends and sew ribbed seam closed. Press carefully.

# Paisley iPod Case

This iPod case is a useful gift to make. The lining ensures that the surface of your phone or iPod won't get scratched and it covers up any thread ends. Felted fabric is lovely to embroider on and the thick fabric provides great protection for valuable items. Make the embroidery as simple or as elaborate as you like.

**Size**
8 x 13 cm (3 x 5 in)

**Materials**
1 x 50 g (2 oz) ball Wash+Filz-it!" dark grey felting yarn
Pair of 5 mm (US 8) knitting needles
Piece of fabric 14 x 19 cm (5½ x 7½ in), for lining
Stranded embroidery cotton, royal purple, bright green, bright blue, dark blue, pale green

Embroidery and sewing needles
Chalk pencil
Sewing thread
Fray stopper (optional)
Sewing machine (optional)

# IPOD CASE

**1** Knit the dark grey yarn following the instructions on the yarn label.

**2** Felt the fabric according to the manufacturer's instructions. Allow to dry. Cut 1 piece 14 x 19 cm (5½ x 7½ in).

**3** Fold the felted piece in half along the long edge (there will be a 1 cm (³/₈ in) seam allowance, which you can trim once sewn). Using the chalk pencil, sketch the paisley shape in the centre of one side.

**4** Work two rows of stem stitch 3 mm (¹/₈ in) apart to outline the paisley motif using purple embroidery cotton. Work padded satin stitch using purple embroidery cotton over the outline.

**5** Using dark blue embroidery cotton, work a line of stem stitch on the outside and inside of the satin stitch.

**6** Draw four arches with chalk pencil in the top third of the paisley. Using bright green embroidery cotton work the arches in stem stitch.

**7** In the circle work a blue flower with a pale green centre. Form a 20-wrap bullion knot into a circle for the centre. Around this work 10 petals each made of 8–13-wrap bullion knots.

**8** Below the flower, work three 20-wrap bullion knot circles, 2 bright green and one bright blue.

**9** Work one bullion knot circle using dark blue in the centre of the paisley motif.

## LINING

**1** Fold the long edge of the lining to the inside and press. If you have a sewing machine, machine stitch the hem, otherwise hand stitch it in place.

**2** Fold the lining right sides together and sew side and bottom seam. Trim the seams but don't turn the right way out.

## EMBROIDERED OUTER

**1** Fold in half and stitch side and bottom seam using the 1 cm (³/₈ in) seam allowance.

**2** Turn the iPod bag right side out. Press corners into shape, and insert the lining. Using matching thread to stitch the case and lining together at the top edges of the bag together.

# Romantic Ruffled Scarf

This is a beautiful ruffled scarf, made with a very soft luxurious yarn containing cashmere. The edging is crocheted with fine kid silk mohair. Beginner knitters could manage this scarf with ease.

### Size
110 x 17 cm (43 x 6¾ in)

### Tension
24 sts and 42 rows to 10 cm (4 in) square when worked in garter st on 4 mm (US 6) knitting needles.

If the tension is too loose the scarf will be limp. Adjust the needle size up if tension is loose and down a size if tension is too tight.

### Materials
3 x 50 g (2 oz) balls of Cascade 220 Superwash Sport DK (8 ply), dark grey

1 x 25 g (1 oz) ball Grignasco Kid Silk Five, pale blue

Pair of 4 mm (US 6) knitting needles

3 mm (US 2½) crochet hook

Wool needle, for sewing up

# SCARF

**Note**: To prevent holes appearing in work when making turnings in short rows, with yarn at the back, slip the next st as if to purl, and bring the yarn to the front. Return the slipped st to the left needle, take the yarn back between the needles and turn the work.

Using 4 mm knitting needles and dark grey, cast on 30 sts.

**Row 1**: Knit.

**Row 2**: K10, turn, knit to end.

**Row 3**: K5, turn, knit to end.

Repeat these 3 rows until work measures 110 cm (43 in), or desired length.

Cast off.

## PICOT EDGE

Using 3 mm crochet hook and pale blue, insert hook into the corner edge of scarf and work 1dc, *3 ch, 1dc into next row end, repeat from * all the way around the scarf.

Sew in all ends carefully. Do not press.

# Lavender Drawer Sachets

What better way to keep your linen cupboard or drawers smelling sweetly than to pop in one or two of these lavender sachets? They are simple to knit in cotton, and if you embroider a lavender motif on the front they would also make lovely gifts.

**Size**
11 x 10 cm (4½ x 4 in)

**Materials**
1 x 50 g (2 oz) ball DK (8-ply) cotton
Pair of 3 mm (US 2/3) knitting needles
1 large decorative button
1 packet delica beads, size 11, dark purple
Stranded embroidery cotton in mauve, medium purple, bright purple and sage green
Wool needle
Beading needle
Sewing thread
Dried lavender flowerheads
25 cm (10 in) of 1 cm (⅜ in) wide purple velvet ribbon
Fabric marker

# LAVENDER SACHET

Using 3 mm knitting needles and DK (8-ply) cotton, cast on 1 st. Working in moss st, inc 1 st at the beg of each row until there are 27 sts. Continue in moss stitch without further shaping until work measures 26 cm (10½ in). Cast off.

## EMBROIDERY

1 Draw a 6 cm (2¼ in) diameter circle approximately 10 cm (4 in) from the cast-on edge.

2 Using three strands of medium purple and bright purple, work whipped chain stitch around the drawn outline.

3 Around the outside of whipped chain stitch, work an outline in stem stitch using three strands of bright purple.

4 Work the lavender motif in the centre of the circle. Using 3 strands of sage green embroidery cotton, stitch the lavender stems using stem stitch.

5 Make clusters of lazy daisy stitch at the base of the stems for the leaves.

6 Embroider two bullion knots, side by side, for each flower: use the lighter purple thread for the upper flowers and the darker shade for the lower flowers.

## RIBBON

Tie the ribbon into a bow and stitch in place diagonally across one corner.

## To Make Up

1 With right sides together fold the bottom edge up 9 cm (3½ in) and sew side seams together using back stitch. Turn right side out.

2 Three-quarters fill with dried lavender flowerheads and stitch the top seam closed. Slip stitch the pointed flap closed.

3 Sew the decorative button over the point of the flap.

# Blue Roses Scarf

This is a great project for novice knitters to learn how to twist yarns into the design. Two beautiful crocheted roses transform this stripy knit. Be sure to carry the yarn not in use up the side of the work and twist it in with the colour being used, this way it will not look loopy along the edge.

### Size
170 x 25 cm (66 x 10 in)

### Tension
22 sts and 30 rows to 10 cm (4 in) square measured over st st on 4.5 mm (US 7) needles using Grignasco Merino Gold DK (8-ply) yarn

### Materials
3 x 50 g (2 oz) balls Grignasco Merino Gold DK (8-ply), light blue

3 x 50 g (2 oz) balls Grignasco Merino Gold DK (8-ply), dark blue

Pair of 4.5 mm (US 7) knitting needles

3 mm (US 2½ ) crochet hook

Wool needle, for finishing

# SCARF

Using 4.5 mm knitting needles and dark blue, cast on 55 sts. Work 6 rows K1, P1 rib.

**Next row**: Join in light blue, knit 1 row.

**Next row**: K2, P to last 2 sts, K2.

Rep these 2 rows in dark blue.

Rep the last 4 rows once and then first 2 rows once.

Cont in stripes of 4 rows dark blue and 4 rows light blue, maintaining garter st border until work measures 165 cm (65 in), ending with a dark blue stripe.

**Next**: Work 2-stripe pattern as for beg, commencing with light blue stripe. *Note: there will be six 2-row stripes at this end.

Change to K1, P1 rib and work 6 rows.

Cast off in rib.

Darn in all loose ends. Press lightly.

## ROSES

Make 2 in dark blue.

Using 3 mm crochet hook and dark blue, make 48 ch. Turn and miss 4 ch, dtr into next 43 ch, tr into last ch.

**Next row**: 3 ch, 3 dtr into each dtr, to last 2 sts, 1 tr, sl into last tr.

Fasten off.

Starting at the end with the sl st and tr crochet, roll the rose up, securing with small stitches at the base.

Stitch the roses to the lower end of the scarf, just above the rib.

# Hyacinth Pin Cushion

*This delightful gift is perfect for a gran or aunt who loves to sew. Bright and colourful fun crocheted flowers adorn the top of the pin cushion, while simple embroidered stitches are used to add interest to the sides design.*

## Size
5 x 10 cm (2 x 4 in)

## Materials
1 x 50 g (2 oz) ball of Wash+Filz-It! cream felting yarn

Pair of 5 mm (US 8) knitting needles

Small amounts of 4-ply wool, mid blue, dark blue, bright green

3 mm (US 11) crochet hook

2 x 2.25 mm (US 1) double-pointed knitting needles

Stranded embroidery cotton, light blue, mid blue, dark blue, sage green

46 x 8 mm (¼ in) pearl beads, cream

Small beads, mid blue, blue

5 x 1 cm (⅜ in) pale blue crystal beads, for flower centre

Sewing needle

Beading needle

Sewing thread

Polyester fibre filling

Plastic pellets

Cardboard circle (slight smaller diameter than base)

Erasable marking pen

1 Using 5 mm (¼ in) knitting needles and cream felting yarn, cast on 50 sts and knit in rows to end of yarn.

2 Felt the piece according to the manufacturer's instruction, then allow to dry. Cut one piece 23 x 4 cm (9 x 1¾ in) for the sides. Cut one top and one base each 8 cm (3 in) diameter. Whip stitch around the edge of each piece by hand.

# EMBROIDERED SIDES

There are three groups of hyacinths around the side panel with three hyacinths in each group. Large green stems and leaves emerges through the middle and to the sides of each group.

1 Use three strands of embroidery cotton throughout. Beginning with the darkest shade of blue and graduating to the lightest shade at the bottom, stitch a mass of tightly clustered French knots to make the hyacinth groups on the side panel.

2 Add long straight stitches for the leaves and stems.

3 Using a beading needle and sewing thread, sew the small blue beads randomly along the side panel.

4 Sew the pearl beads around the bottom edge of the pin cushion and the blue beads around the top edge of the pin cushion.

5 Make up as for Rose and Daisy Pin Cushion using three strands of mid blue embroidery cotton throughout.

## LEAVES
## Make 7

Using 2.25 mm knitting needles and 4-ply bright green, cast on 3 sts, work an I-cord for 1.5 cm

**Row 1**: (RS) Knit.

**Row 2 and all even rows**: Knit.

**Row 3**: K1, m1, K1, m1, K1.

**Row 5**: K2, m1, K1, m1, K2.

**Row 7**: K3 m1, K1, m1, K3.

**Row 9**: K4, m1, K1, m1, K4.

**Row 11**: Knit

**Row 13**: Sl 1, K1, psso, K7, k2tog.

**Row 15**: Sl 1, K1, psso, K5, k2tog.

**Row 17**: Sl 1, K1, psso, K3, k2tog.

**Row 19**: Sl 1, K1, psso, K1, k2tog.

**Row 21**: S1, k2tog, psso.

Fasten off.

## FLOWERS
## Make 6

Using 3 mm crochet hook and dark blue 4-ply, make 4 ch, join with a ss, into a ring.

**Round 1**: (RS) 2ch, 9 dc in ring with dark blue, ss to top of 2ch (10 sts).

**Round 2**: Using contrast blue 5ch, 1 tr tr in each of next 9 dc, ss to top of 5ch. Fasten off.
Darn in ends and form into a neat circle.
Alternate the centre colour of the flower so that you use mid blue for three flowers and dark blue for three flowers. Sew a blue crystal bead to each flower before attaching to pin cushion.

## To Make Up

Sew one leaf in the centre of the pin cushion and then arrange the remainder of the leaves and flowers around the top and stitch firmly into place.

*Hyacinth pin cushion* / 145

# Fathers' Day Socks

Hand-knitted socks can be tailored to fit the foot and are so warm and comfortable. These will last for many years. This is a fairly basic pattern, which you can personalise with stripes or by changing the rib pattern.

## Size
To fit foot length 25, 27, 28 cm (10, 10½, 11 in).

## Materials
1 x 100 g (3½ oz) ball Cherry Tree Hill Sock Wool, Sockittome, chocolate brown
2 x 50 g (2 oz) balls Malabrigo Lace Superwash, coffee/toffee
Set of 4 x 2.75 mm (US 2) double-pointed knitting needles
Wool needle, for grafting toe

## Tension
34 sts and 46 rows to 10 cm (4 in) square when worked over st st using Malabrigo yarn on 2.75 mm (US 2) needles

Note: Rib, heels and toes are worked in Cherry Hill yarn. Body of sock is worked in Malabrigo Lace Superwash

## Make 2

Using 3 x 2.75 mm knitting needles and Cherry Hill yarn, cast on 72 sts (24, 24, 24). Join into a ring, being careful not to twist sts.

Work in K1, P1 rib for 10 cm (4 in). Break off yarn and join in new colour.

Work in st st (every round knit) for 10 cm (4 in).

### Leg Shaping

**Next round**: First needle, K1, K2tog to end of needle; Second needle, Knit; Third needle, Knit to last 3 sts, sl 1, K1, psso.

Knit the next 6 rounds.

Rep these 7 rounds twice more (21 sts) on first and third needles, 24 sts on second needle.

Cont in st st until work measures 28 cm from beg.

### Divide for Heel

**Next round**: K17, sl last 17 sts of round on to other end of same needle (these 34 sts are for heel). Divide rem sts between two needles and leave for instep. Heel sts will be worked backwards and forwards in rows.

**Row 1**: Sl 1, purl to end.

**Row 2**: *Sl 1, K1, rep from * to last st, K1.

Rep these 2 rows another 8 times and then first row once.

### Turn Heel

K19, k2tog, K1, turn, P6, p2tog, P1, turn, K7, k2tog, K1, turn, P8, p2tog, P1, turn, K9, k2tog, K1, turn, P10, p2tog, P1, turn, K11, k2tog, K1, turn, Cont in this manner until all sts are worked on to one needle. Knit back 10 sts, completing heel. Slip all instep sts on to one needle.

Beg at centre of heel; First needle K10, pick up and K17 sts along side of heel; Second needle, K across instep sts; Third needle, pick up and K17 sts along other side of heel and rem 10 heel sts.

### Shape Instep

**Round 1**: First needle, knit to last 4 sts, k2tog, K2; Second needle, Knit; Third needle, K2, sl 1, K1, psso, K to end.

**Round 2**: Knit.

Repeat these two rounds until 16 sts rem on first and third needles and 32 sts remain on second needle.

Continue without further shaping until foot measures 15, 17, 19 cm (6 6½,7½ in) from where sts were picked up at side of instep.

### Shape Toe

**Round 1**: First needle, K to last 4 sts, k2tog, K2; Second needle, K2, sl 1, K1, psso, K to last 4 sts, k2tog, K2; Third needle, K2, sl 1, K1, psso, K to end.

**Round 2**: Knit.

Repeat these two rounds until there are 7 sts rem on first and third needles and 14 sts on second needle. Divide sts evenly on to two needles.

## Graft Toe

See Grafting Knitting in Essential Techniques.

# Lacy Towel Edging

This lovely lace edging is quick to knit and can be used to decorate all kinds of clothes as well as accessories. A lace edging adds a luxurious touch to these towels making them suitable for guest rooms.

## Tension
If you have not knitted on very fine needles or with knitting cotton, knit a sample first to get used to the feel of the cotton in your hands.

## Materials
1 hand towel
1 bath towel
Pair 1 mm (US 000) knitting needles
1 x 50 g (2 oz) ball of knitting cotton
Matching thread
Sewing needle
1.5 m x 2 cm (¾ in) wide ribbon

## Special Abbreviations
**M1**: All worked as a yfwd.
**M2**: Pick up the loop that lies between the two needles for the first M1, and then ytwd, for the second M1. Where you have a M1 following a purl stitch be sure to wrap the yarn all the way around the needle.

## KNITTED LACE

Make 1 for each towel, to fit across the top when slightly stretched

Using 1 mm knitting needles and knitting cotton, cast on 25 sts.

**Row 1**: Knit.

**Row 2**: Sl 1, K2, m1, k2tog, K1, m1, k2tog, K2, m1, k2tog, K5, m1, k2tog, K1, (m2, k2tog) twice, K1.

**Row 3**: K3, P1, K2, P1, K3, m1, k2tog, K12, m1, k2tog, K1.

**Row 4**: Sl 1, K2, m1, k2tog, (K2, m1, k2tog) twice, K4, m1, k2tog, K3, (m2, K2tog) twice, K1.

**Row 5**: K3, P1, K2, P1, K5, m1, k2tog, K12, m1, k2tog, K1.

**Row 6**: Sl 1, K2, m1, k2tog, K3, m1, k2tog, K2, m1, k2tog, K3, m1, k2tog, K5, (m2, K2tog) twice, K1.

**Row 7**: K3, P1, K2, P1, K7, m1, k2tog, K12, m1, k2tog, K1.

**Row 8**: Sl 1, K2, m1, k2tog, K4, (m1, k2tog, K2) twice, m1, k2tog, K12.

**Row 9**: Cast off 6 sts, K7, m1, k2tog, K12, m1, k2tog, K1.

Repeat rows 2–9 until required length is achieved ending with a row 9. Cast off.

## To Make Up

Press lightly and darn in loose ends neatly. Position lace panel (right side has a slightly more ridged appearance). Carefully hand stitch in place along the top edge and down the sides using a tiny stitch. Place the ribbon on top of the lace, turning in 5 mm (¼ in) at each end to prevent fraying. Stitch in place.

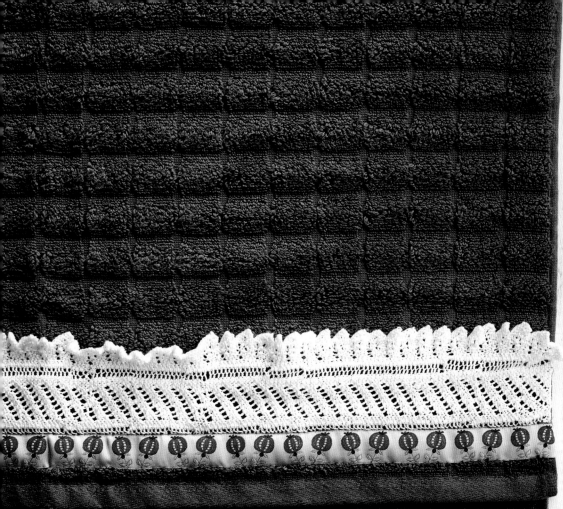

# Crocheted Daisy Chain Edging

This lovely crocheted daisy border can be applied to lots of different items to give a pretty and delicate finish. Surrounding a pristine white face flannel it would make a beautiful gift for a new baby. The border can be adapted to any size. You will need a little extra length for each corner so complete row one and ensure that it is long enough to go right around your item before commencing row two.

## Materials

White face flannel
1 x 50 g (2 oz) ball Grignasco Cotton 5
1.75 mm (US 2) crochet hook
Stranded embroidery cotton, pale pink, dark pink, bright green

Embroidery needle
White sewing thread
Sewing needle
Chalk pencil

# DAISY BORDER

Using 1.75 mm crochet hook and Grignasco Cotton 5, make 4 ch.

**Row 1**: 2 tr, into 4ch from hook, 4ch (2 tr, 3ch, ss, 3ch, 2 tr) all into 4ch from hook, * 9ch, 2 tr, into fourth ch from hook, 4ch, (2 tr, 3ch, ss, 3ch, 2 tr) all into fourth ch from hook; rep from * for number of daisies required, do not turn.

**Row 2**: Working along the base of row 1 to complete the daisies, 3ch, ss, into same place as the other petals for first daisy, (3ch, 2 tr, 3ch, ss) all in to the same place, 3ch, ss into top edge of last petal of this daisy* 8ch (2 tr, 3ch, ss, 3ch) three times all into fourth ch from hook, (2 tr, 3ch, ss) all into same place, 4ch, ss into top edge of first petal of next daisy, 3ch, ss into centre of this daisy, (3ch, 2 tr, 3ch, ss) all into same place, 3ch, ss into top edge of last petal of this daisy; rep from * to end.

## To Make Up

Darn in all ends. Press carefully under a damp cloth using a warm iron, if necessary. Beginning at the centre of one side, carefully stitch the daisy chain border in place, gathering slightly at the corners. Use matching thread to match the flannel and the border and use very small stitches, particularly at the corners.

## Embroidery

Many flannels have a section where the pile has not been cut and it is easiest to work the embroidery here.

1 Mark the position of the centre rose first with the chalk pencil, then the required number to each side.

2 Work the centre of the bullion roses first with 3 strands of darker pink embroidery cotton and two 7-wrap bullion knots. Finish off neatly as the back will show. Finish each individual rose separately. Don't try to carry the cotton across to a new rose.

3 With 3 strands of pale pink embroidery cotton work 5-wrap bullion knots overlapping each other around the central two. Each bullion wrap should have 9–11 wraps.

4 Finally using 3 strands of embroidery cotton and lazy daisy stitch work a pair of bright green leaves so that they sit above the rose.

# Crocheted Lavender Bag

This little lavender sachet comprises eight crocheted lace squares, which are stitched together. Inside is an organza bag containing lavender. Make this gift one that you can make while on the go; the squares can be made individually and then put together when you have a spare moment.

**Size**
10 x 10 cm (4 x 4 in)

**Materials**
1 x 50 g (2 oz) ball of Grignasco Cotton 5
1.75 mm (US 2) crochet hook
Wool needle
20 x 10 cm (8 x 4 in) pink organza, or other very lightweight fabric
Dried lavender flowerheads
Matching thread
Sewing needle
Sewing machine (optional)

# CROCHETED SQUARES

## Make 8

Using 1.75 mm crochet hook and Grignasco Cotton 5, make 6ch and join with a ss to form a ring.

**Round 1**: 1ch, 2 dc into a ring, (7ch, 4 dc into ring) 3 times, 7ch, 2 dc into ring, ss into top of first dc.

**Round 2**: *(1 dc, 8 tr, 1 dc) all into 7ch loop, ss into second of 4 dc between loops; rep from * 3 times more.

**Round 3**: Ss into first dc and second tr of loop, 1ch, 1 dc into same place, 2ch, miss 1 tr, (1 tr, 3ch, 1 tr) all into next tr, 2ch, miss 1 tr, 1dc into next tr, 5ch, *miss 1 dc and 1 tr of next loop, 1 dc into second tr, 2ch, miss 1 tr, (1 tr, 3ch, 1 tr) all into next tr, 2ch, miss 1 tr, 1 dc into next tr, 5ch; rep from *twice more, ss into top of first dc.

**Round 4**: 1ch, *1 dc into dc, 2 dc into 2ch space, 1 dc into tr, (2 dc, 3ch, 2 dc) into 3ch space at corner, 1 dc into tr, 2 dc in 2ch space, 1 dc into dc, 5 dc into 5ch space; rep from * 3 times, ss into top of first dc.

**Round 5**: 1ch, *1 dc into each of the next dc, (2 dc, 3ch, 2 dc) into 3ch space at corner, 1 dc into each of next 11 dc; rep from * 3 times, ss into top of first dc.

Fasten off.

## To Make Up

**1** Darn in all ends. Press under a damp cloth and block to shape, if needed.

**2** Sew 4 squares together using mattress stitch to make each side of the bag.

**3** With wrong sides together and using mattress stitch sew around three sides of the bag.

## ORGANZA BAG

**1** Fold the organza into a square and stitch around the raw edges, using a 1 cm (³/₈ in) seam allowance. If sewing by hand use very small stitches. Leave an opening for turning the bag right side out.

**2** Trim seams and finish edges using zigzag stitch to prevent fraying. Turn right side out.

**3** Fill bag with dried lavender flowerheads and hand stitch the opening closed using very small stitches.

**4** Place the lavender bag inside the crocheted bag and sew the top seam closed.

# Baby Bloomer

This little set of vest and matching undies is ideal for keeping baby warm in winter. The vest top is a simple knit embellished with delicate bullion-knot roses. It is stretchy enough to fit over a tiny head without the need for buttons. The knickers have simple, short row shaping at the back to accommodate a nappy.

### Size
To fit: 0 (3 months, 6 months)

### Tension
29 sts and 38.5 rows to 10 cm (4 in) square when measured over st st using 3.25 mm (US 3) knitting needles

### Materials
*For the vest:* 2, (3, 3) x 25 g (1 oz) balls of Heirloom 4-ply Silk and Wool mix, cream
*For the knickers:* 3, (3, 4) x 25 g (1 oz) balls of Heirloom 4-ply Silk or Wool, cream

Pair of 2.75 mm (US 2) knitting needles
Pair of 3.25 mm (US 3) knitting needles
Wool needle, for sewing up
2 stitch holders
Stranded embroidery cotton, light blue, dark blue, sage and bright green
1 m x 1.5 cm (40 x ½ in) wide satin ribbon, bright blue
Embroidery needle

# VEST

## Make 2

Using 2.75 mm knitting needles and cream 4-ply,
cast on 53, (61, 67) sts.

**Row 1**: K2, *P1, K1, rep from * to last st, K1.

**Row 2**: K1, *P1, K1, rep from * to end.

Rep rows 1 and 2 six times (14 rows rib in total).
Change to 3.25 mm knitting needles and st st.
Work in st st until work measures 13, 15, 17 cm
(5, 6, 6½ in) from beg.

## SHAPE ARMHOLES

Cast of 4, (5, 5) sts at the beg of next 2 rows.
Work another 17, (19, 21) rows without shaping.

## SHAPE NECK

**Next row**: K16, (19, 22) turn.

** Work on these 16, (19, 22) sts.

Cont in st st, dec 1 st at neck edge on every
row until 12, (15, 18) sts rem, then on alt rows
until 11 (13, 15) sts rem. Work another 5 rows
without shaping.

## SHAPE SHOULDER

Cast off 4, (4, 5) sts at beg of next row and foll
alt row. Work one row. Cast off rem 3 (5, 5) sts**.
Slip central 13 sts onto a stitch holder.
Re-join yarn to rem sts and knit to end. Rep
from ** to ** working 6 rows instead of 5 before
shoulder shaping.

## NECKBAND

Using back stitch, join right shoulder seam. With
right side facing and using 2.75 mm knitting
needles, pick up and K73, (81, 89) sts evenly
around neck including sts from stitch holders.
Work 5 rows rib as before beg with row 2.

## ARMHOLE BANDS

Using back stitch, join left shoulder and
neckband seam. With right side facing and using
2.75 mm knitting needles, pick up and knit 67,
(77, 85) sts along armhole edge. Work 5 rows rib
as before beg with row 2.

## To Make Up

Using back stitch, join side and armhole seams.
Press vest carefully, including seams using a
damp cloth.

## EMBROIDERED DECORATION

Use three strands of embroidery cotton, work
one bullion knot rose on the vest centre front
just under the ribbed neckband. Work another
rose at each side of the first one. Start each new
wrap approximately one-third of the way along
the previous knot to create a rounded shape.
Work another bullion rose on the lower left side,
just above the ribbed band (see Techniques).
Work a row of whipped chain stitch around
the front neckline using 3 strands of green
embroidery cotton. Use the paler green for the

chain stitch and whip the chain with the brighter green. Be careful not to pull the embroidery too tightly or it may decrease the stretchiness of the neckline.

# KNICKERS
## BACK
Using 3.25 mm knitting needles and 4-ply yarn, cast on 19, (21, 23) sts.
Work in st st, inc 1 st at each end of every row until there are 73, (83, 85) sts.
Work another 49 (49, 52)** rows st st without shaping.

### SHAPE BACK
Note: To avoid holes in work in short row shaping, when turning, bring yarn to front of work, slip next st, onto right-hand needle, yarn back, sl st back on to left-hand needle, then turn and cont with instructions.

**Row 1**: Knit to last 8 sts, turn.
**Row 2**: Purl to last 8 sts, turn.
**Row 3**: Knit to last 16 sts, turn.
**Row 4**: Purl to last 16 sts, turn.
**Row 5**: Knit to last 24 sts, turn.
**Row 6**: Purl to last 24 sts, turn.
**Row 7**: Knit to last 32 sts, turn.
**Row 8**: Purl to last 32 sts, turn.
**Row 9**: Knit to end.
**Row 10**: Purl.
**Row 11**: *** K2, *P1, K1, rep from * to end.

**Row 12**: K1, *P1, K1, rep from * to end.
Rep rows 11 and 12 twice more.
**Eyelet row**: K2, *yfwd, k2tog, rep from * to last st, K1.
Work 5 rows rib.
Cast off in rib.***

## FRONT
Work as for back to **
Work 2 rows st st.
Work as for back from *** to ***.

## LEG BANDS
Press pieces carefully under a damp cloth. With right sides together join one side seam using back stitch.
With right sides facing and using 2.75 mm knitting needles, pick up and K57, (61, 65) sts around leg hole. Work 7 rows K1, P1 rib. Cast off in rib.

Using back stitch join crotch seam. Work second leg hole as for first and then with right sides together join side seam.
Thread satin ribbon through eyelet holes.
On left side, 3 cm (1¼ in) below rib waistband work a bullion knot rose using darker blue for the two central knots and paler blue for the outer petals. Use pale green embroidery thread to make lazy daisy leaves and French knots

# Ballerina Slippers

These sweet little slippers are perfect for a special occasion. With their little ties, lacy edging and embroidered rose they would make a beautiful addition to a christening outfit.

## Size
Sole: 7 cm (2¾ in) long

## Materials
1 x 25 g (1 oz) ball of 4-ply Heirloom Pure Wool Baby, pale pink
Set of 4 x 2.25 mm (US 1) double-pointed knitting needles
3 mm (US 11) crochet hook
Wool needle, for sewing up
Pale pink and medium pink stranded embroidery cotton
Sewing needle

# SLIPPERS

## Make 2

Using two 2.25 mm (US 1) double-pointed knitting needles and 4-ply yarn, cast on 7 sts.

**Row 1**: Knit

**Row 2**: Knit

**Row 3**: K1, inc in next st, knit to last 3 sts, inc in next st, K2.

**Row 4**: Knit.

Rep rows 3 and 4 until there are 15 sts.

Cont in garter st (every row knit) until work measures 6.5 cm (2½ in).

**Next row**: K1, k2tog, knit to last 3 sts, k2tog, K1.

**Next row**: Knit.

Rep these last two rows until 5 sts rem to complete the sole.

With these 5 sts on needle, pick up and K28 sts down first side of foot to the centre of the toe onto same needle. Take another needle and pick up and K29 sts along the other side of the foot ending at the 5 original sts. Slip the original 5 sts onto a third needle (28, 5, 29); (the centre stitch of the 5 is the beginning of the round.)

**Round 1**: Purl

**Round 2**: K25, k2tog, K8, sl 1, K1, psso, K25.

**Round 3**: Purl.

**Round 4**: K24, k2tog, K8, sl 1, K1, psso, K24

**Round 5**: Purl.

**Round 6**: K23, k2tog, K8, sl 1, K1, psso, K23.

**Round 7**: Purl.

**Round 8**: K22, k2tog, K8, sl 1, K1, psso, K22.

**Round 9**: Purl.

**Round 10**: K21, (k2tog) 3 times, (sl 1, K1, psso) 3 times, K21.

**Round 11**: Purl.

**Round 12**: K18, (k2tog) 3 times, (sl 1, K1, psso) 3 times, K18.

**Round 13**: Purl.

**Round 14**: K15, (k2tog) 3 times, (sl 1, K1, psso) 3 times, K15.

**Round 15**: Purl.

Cast off.

## CROCHET EDGING

Using 3 mm (US 11) crochet hook and 4-ply yarn, make a length of chain, (in multiples of 3) long enough to go around the opening of the slipper, plus 2 extra ch.

**Row 1**: 1 dc, into second ch from hook, 1 dc into each ch to end.

**Row 2**: 1ch, 1 dc into first dc, *5ch, miss 2 dc, 1 dc into next dc, rep from * to end.

**Row 3**: 1ch, (3 dc, 3ch, 3 dc) into each 5ch sp to end. Fasten off.

Darn in loose ends and press flat with warm iron under a damp cloth. Do not stretch.

Stitch edging in place around the opening of the slipper.

## I-CORD TIES

Using 2.25 mm (US 1) double-pointed knitting needles and 4-ply yarn, cast on 3 sts.

**Row 1**: *K3, do not turn, slide sts to other end of needle, pull yarn firmly behind work, rep from * until I-cord measures 45 cm (17 in).

To cast off sl 1, k2tog, psso, fasten off.

Darn in all loose ends.

Fold in half and stitch fold to back of slipper.

## EMBROIDERED ROSEBUD

Using three strands of embroidery cotton, make a bullion knot rosebud on top of instep. Using medium pink, place two 7-wrap bullion knots parallel to each other. Make five light pink 9–11-wrap bullion knots around these, central knots, overlapping the knots slightly in the same way that petals overlap.

*Ballerina slippers* / 165

# Newborn Penguin Slippers and Hat

This is a hat and slipper set for a new baby. It is a simple knit using supersoft yarn – a perfect gift for a winter baby.

## Size
*Hat*
To fit: 3–6 months
*Slippers*
3–6 months (sole measures 7.5 cm/3 in)

## Materials
*Slippers*
1 x 25 g (1 oz) ball 4-ply pure wool, cream
1 x 25 g (1 oz) ball 4-ply pure wool, dark grey
Set of 4 x 2.25 mm (US 1) double-pointed knitting needles

2 penguin buttons
Wool needle, for sewing up
Sewing thread and needle

*Hat*
1 x 50 g (2 oz) ball DK (8-ply) wool, cream
1 x 50 g (2 oz) ball DK (8-ply) wool, dark grey
Pair of 4 mm (US 6) knitting needles
2 x 2.75 mm (US 2) double-pointed knitting needles
Small amount polyester fibre filling

# SLIPPERS

## Make 2

Using 2 x 2.25 mm double-pointed knitting needles and dark grey 4-ply, cast on 7 sts.

**Row 1**: Knit

**Row 2**: Knit

**Row 3**: K1, inc in next st, knit to last 3 sts, inc in next st, K2.

**Row 4**: Knit.

Rep rows 3 and 4 until there are 15 sts.

Cont in garter st (every row knit) until work measures 6.5 cm (2½ in)

**Next row**: K1, k2tog, knit to last 3 sts, k2tog, K1.

**Next row**: Knit.

Rep these last two rows until 5 sts rem. Break off dark grey and join in cream.

With these 5 sts on the needle, pick up and K28 sts onto same needle to the centre of the toe. Take another needle and pick up and K29 sts along the other side of the foot ending at the 5 original sts. It is easier at this point to slip the five original sts onto a third needle (28, 5, 29). (The centre st of the 5 is the beginning of the round.)

**Round 1**: Purl

**Round 2**: K25, k2tog, K8, sl 1, K1, psso, K25.

**Round 3**: Purl.

**Round 4**: K24, k2tog, K8, sl 1, K1, psso, K24.

**Round 5**: Purl.

**Round 6**: K23, k2tog, K8, sl 1, K1, psso, K23.

**Round 7**: Purl.

**Round 8**: K22, k2tog, K8, sl 1, K1, psso, K22.

**Round 9**: Purl.

**Round 10**: K21, (k2tog) 3 times, sl 1, K1, psso 3 times, K21.

**Round 11**: Purl.

**Round 12**: K18, (k2tog) 3 times, sl 1, K1, psso 3 times, K18.

**Round 13**: Purl.

**Round 14**: K15, (k2tog) 3 times, sl 1, K1, psso 3 times, K15.

**Round 15**: Purl.

Cast off.

Darn in all loose ends. Sew penguin button on the toe of slipper.

## HAT

Using 4 mm knitting needles and dark grey DK (8-ply), cast on 80 sts. Work 10 rows st st. Break off dark grey and join in cream DK (8-ply). Cont in garter st until work measures 15 cm (6 in) from beg.

### Crown Shaping

**Next row**: *K6, k2tog, rep from * to end.

**Next row**: Knit.

**Next row**: *K5, k2tog, rep from * to end.

**Next row**: Knit.

**Next row**: *K4, k2tog, rep from * to end.

**Next row**: Knit.

**Next row**: *K3, k2tog, rep from * to end.

**Next row**: Knit.

**Next row**: *K2, k2tog, rep from * to end.

**Next row**: Knit.

**Next row**: *K1, k2tog, rep from * to end.

**Next row**: Knit.

**Next row**: *K2tog, rep from * to end.

Break off yarn, thread through rem sts. Pull up tightly and fasten off. Darn in all ends. Allow brim to roll to the outside.

## Top Knot Ball

Using 2.75 mm double-pointed knitting needles and dark grey DK (8 ply), cast on 12 sts.

**Row 1**: Knit

**Row 2**: P10, wrap.

**Row 3**: K8, wrap.

**Row 4**: P6, wrap.

**Row 5**: K4, wrap.

**Row 6**: Purl.

Rep these 6 rows another 4 times. Cast off. With right sides together sew side seam half way. Turn right side out and stuff firmly. Sew the rest of the seam and then run a gathering thread around the cast-on edge. Pull up firmly and fasten off. Do the same with the other end. Sew the ball to the top of the hat.

# Pretty Handkerchiefs

This beautiful lace edging is crocheted directly onto a linen handkerchief. The second handkerchief has three blue bullion knot flowers embroidered with one strand of embroidery cotton, making it a perfect gift for a bride-to-be.

## Materials

2 linen handkerchiefs,
   25 x 25 cm (10 x 10 in)
1 x 50 g (2 oz) ball of no. 40
   Cebelia crochet cotton
1.75 mm (US 4) steel crochet
   hook
stranded embroidery cotton,
   2 shades of blue
Embroidery needle
Darning needle

## CROCHET EDGING

The edging is worked directly onto the handkerchief. Tension is important when crocheting with cotton. Too tight and the work will not sit flat and too loose and your work will not have any definition. If you have not crocheted with fine cotton before you might like to make a practice sample first before you work your piece.

**Row 1**: Attach crochet cotton 1.5 cm (½ in) to the left side of one corner and work dc along edge of handkerchief, working 3 dc into each corner. Join with a ss into first dc.

**Row 2**: 3ch, miss 2 dc, 1 tr into next dc, 6ch, 1 tr into top of last tr, (a cross st made) *5ch, miss 4 dc, thread over hook twice, insert hook into next dc and draw thread through as for a dbl tr, (4 loops on hook), thread over and draw through 2 loops, thread over, miss 2 dc, insert hook into next dc and draw hook through (5 loops on hook), thread over and draws through 2 loops at a time (4 times), 4 ch, 1 tr into joining at centre of cross completing cross repeat from *. Making 2 cross sts closely together at corners join last 5 ch with ss to third of 6ch of first cross st.

**Row 3**: 6ch, *1 tr into next leg of same cross st, 3ch, 1 dc into 5ch sp, 3ch, 1 tr into first leg of next cross st, 3ch: repeat from * joining last 3ch into third of 6ch first made.

**Row 4**: 1 ss into sp, 5ch, 1 tr into same sp, 2ch, 1 tr into same sp * 3ch, 1 dc into next dc, 3ch, into next sp, work 1 tr, 2ch, 1 tr, 2ch and 1 tr: repeat from * joining last 3ch with ss to third of 5ch.

Fasten off. Darn in ends carefully and press.

## EMBROIDERED HANDKERCHIEF

**Note**: Edging is worked directly onto handkerchief.

**Row 1**: Attach cotton 1 cm (³/₈ in) to the left of one corner and work dc along edge of handkerchief, working 3 dc into each corner. Join with a sl st into first dc.

**Row 2**: 3ch, (to count as a tr), *miss 2 dc, 1 tr into next dc, 4ch, 1 dbl tr into each of next 3 dc leaving the last loop of each on hook. Thread over and draw through all loops on hook (cluster made), 4ch, 1 tr into next dc: repeat from * along row making a cluster at corners. Join last 4ch with a ss to third of 3ch first made. There should be an uneven number of clusters on each side, plus 1 at each corner.

**Row 3**: 1 ss into each of next 2ch of 4ch loop, 1 dc into same loop, *4ch, 1 dc into next 4ch loop, 6ch. 1 dc into next loop; repeat from * along row, making 6 ch loops over clusters at corners. Join last 6ch to first dc made.

**Row 4**: Ss into first 6ch loop *1 dc, 1 htr, 2 tr, 1 dbl tr, 2 tr, 1 htr, 1 dc (all in 6ch sp) 1ch, 1 dc,

1ch, (in 4ch sp), rep from * finishing with sl st
into first dc.
Fasten off. Darn in ends and press.

## Embroidery

Embroider 3 bullion roses in one corner. Each
bullion knot has 12 wraps made using 1 strand
of embroidery cotton.

# Knitted Lace Pillowcase Edging

A velvet ribbon offsets this antique lace edging. If you have an antique-style bed or an old rocking chair this would look very pretty. I have made it in a cream cotton with a dark brown velvet ribbon on a dark cream pillowcase. It would look equally good in pristine white with a ribbon to match the colours in the bedroom.

### Size
To fit: standard pillowcase

### Materials
1 x 300 m (328 yd) ball of Milford Jumbo, Perle no. 10
Pair 1.5 mm (US 000) knitting needles
75 cm (30 in) of 1 cm (⅜ in) wide velvet ribbon, dark brown
Sewing thread
Sewing needle
Standard pillowcase

## LACE EDGING

Using 1.5 mm knitting needles and Milford
Jumbo cast on 8 sts

**Row 1**: Knit.

**Row 2**: Sl 1, K1, (yo, k2tog) twice, yo, K2.

**Row 3**: K2, yo, K2, (yo, k2tog) twice, K1.

**Row 4**: Sl 1, K1, (yo, k2tog) twice, K2, yo, K2.

**Row 5**: K2, yo, K4, (yo k2tog) twice, K1.

**Row 6**: Sl 1, K1, (yo, k2tog) twice, K4, yo, K2.

**Row 7**: K2, yo, K6, (yo, k2tog) twice, K1.

**Row 8**: Sl 1, K1, (yo, k2tog) twice, K6, yo, K2.

**Row 9**: K2, yo, K8, (yo, k2tog) twice, K1.

**Row 10**: Sl 1, K1, (yo, k2tog) twice, K8, yo, K2.

**Row 11**: K2, yo, K10, (yo, k2tog) twice, K1.

**Row 12**: Sl 1, K1, (yo, k2tog) twice, K10, yo, K2.

**Row 13**: Cast off 11 sts, K2, (yo, k2tog) twice, K1.
Repeat rows 2–13 until lace is long enough to fit
along edge of pillowcase ending with a row 13.
Cast off.

## To Make Up

Darn in loose ends. Press lightly, if necessary.
Trim the ribbon to fit the pillowcase leaving
5 mm (¼ in) at each end to hem. Turn the raw
ends of the ribbon to the wrong side and hem.
Stitch the flat edge of the lace panel to the
ribbon using very small stitches. Sew the ribbon
to the pillowcase 10 cm (4 in) below the top
edge using a hemming stitch. Press.

# Simple Striped Beanie

This simple striped beanie is knitted in cheerful reds and blues – perfect for a little boy. The soft cotton yarn will keep its shape when washed and is soft and comfortable for a young child to wear.

## Size
To fit: 12–18 months

## Materials
1 x 50 g (2 oz) ball Patons Serenity DK (8-ply) Cotton, red
1 x 50 g (2 oz) ball Patons Serenity DK (8-ply) Cotton, navy
1 x 50 g (2 oz) ball Patons Serenity DK (8-ply) Cotton, mid blue
Set of 4 x 4 mm (US 6) double-pointed knitting needles
Wool needle, for sewing up

# HAT

Using 3 x 4 mm double-pointed knitting needles and red, cast on 90 sts (30, 30, 30). Join into a ring, being careful not to twist sts.

Work 12 rounds in st st, (every round knit).

Commence stripe pattern as follows: 2 rounds red, 2 rounds navy, 2 rounds mid blue.

Work 7 complete repeats of the stripe patt (42 rounds).

## COMMENCE CROWN SHAPING

Cont in stripe patt

**Round 1**: In red, *K7, k2tog, rep from * to end of round.

**Round 2**: In red, knit.

**Round 3**: In navy, *K6, k2tog, rep from * to end of round.

**Round 4**: In navy, knit.

**Round 5**: In mid blue, *K5, K2tog, rep from * to end of round.

**Round 6**: In mid blue, knit.

**Round 7**: In red, *K4, k2tog, rep from * to end of round.

**Round 8**: In red, knit.

Cont dec in this manner on alt rows and keeping stripe patt correct until the row K1, k2tog has been worked. Finish the rest of the hat in red.

**Next round**: Knit

**Next round**: K2tog all round.

Break off yarn, thread through rem sts, pull up tightly and fasten off.

Darn in all ends. Press lightly and allow brim to roll to the outside.

# I-CORD LOOP

Using two 4 mm double-pointed knitting needles and red DK (8-ply) cotton, cast on 3 sts.

**Row 1**: *Knit. Slide sts to other end of needle, do not turn, pull yarn firmly behind sts, rep from *, until I-cord is 8 cm (3 in) long.

**Next row**: Sl 1, k2tog, psso, fasten off.

Darn in one end. Use the other end to stitch in to a ring. Attach firmly to the top of the hat.

# Stripy Socks

Here is a pair of men's socks in lovely shades of charcoal, crimson, pale grey and cream. These are the perfect gift for an outdoor man, and will keep feet snug and warm on the coldest days.

## Size
To fit men's foot lengths:
  25 cm, 27 cm, 28 cm (10, 10½, 11 in)
Length to heel: 23 cm (9 in), (can be lengthened)

## Materials
2 x 50 g (2 oz) balls of 4-ply sock yarn, charcoal grey
1 x 50 g (2 oz) ball of 4-ply sock yarn, pale grey
1 x 50 g (2 oz) ball of 4-ply sock yarn, crimson
1 x 50 g (2 oz) ball of 4-ply sock yarn, cream

Set of 4 x 2.25 mm (US 2/3) double-pointed knitting needles
Wool needle, for grafting toe

# SOCKS

## Make 2

Using three 2.25 mm double-pointed knitting needles and main colour, cast on 78 sts (26, 26, 26). Join into a ring, being careful not to twist sts.

Work in K1, P1 rib for 8 cm (3 in).

## BEGIN STRIPED PATTERN

**Note**: Striped pattern is worked in st st as follows: 1 row charcoal grey, 1 row pale grey, 1 row crimson, 1 row cream.

Repeat this 4-row patt another 7 times.

Cont in charcoal grey only for calf shaping.

### CALF SHAPING

First needle, K1, k2tog, knit to end of round; Second needle, Knit; Third needle, K to last 3 sts, sl 1, K1, psso, K1.

Knit 4 rounds without shaping.

Rep these 5 rounds another 5 times (66 sts).

### DIVIDE FOR HEEL

**Next round**: K17, slip last 17 sts of round on to other end of same needle (these 34 sts are for heel). Divide rem sts between two needles and leave for instep. Heel sts are worked backwards and forwards in rows. Join contrast colour for the first row of the heel.

**Row 1**: Sl 1, purl to end.

**Row 2**: *Sl 1, K1, rep from * to last st, K1.

Rep these 2 rows another 8 times and then first row once.

### TURN HEEL

K19, k2tog, K1, turn, P6, p2tog, P1, turn, K7, k2tog, K1, turn, P8, p2tog, P1, turn, K9, k2tog, K1, turn, P10, p2tog, P1, turn, K11, k2tog, K1, turn, Cont in this manner until all sts are worked on to one needle. Knit back 10 sts, completing heel. Slip all instep sts on to one needle. Break off contrast colour and join back in main colour

Beg at centre of heel, K10, pick up and K18 sts along side of heel; with second needle, knit across instep sts; with third needle, pick up and K17 sts along other side of heel and rem 10 heel sts.

### SHAPE INSTEP

**Round 1**: First needle, Knit to last 4 sts, k2tog, K2; Second needle, Knit; Third needle, K2, sl 1, K1, psso, K to end.

**Round 2**: Knit.

Repeat these two rounds until there are 16 sts on first and third needles and 32 sts on second needle.

Cont without further shaping until foot measures 15, 17, 19 cm (6, 6½, 7½ in) from point where sts were picked up at side of instep.

### SHAPE TOE

Break off main colour and join in contrast colour.

**Round 1**: First needle, Knit to last 4 sts, k2tog,

K2; Second needle, K2, Sl 1, K1, psso, K to last 4 sts, k2tog, K2; Third needle, K2, sl 1, K1, psso, K to end.

**Round 2**: Knit.

Repeat these two rounds until 7 sts rem on first and third needles and 14 sts on second needle. Divide sts evenly on to two needles.

## To Graft Toe

See Grafting Knitting in Essential Techniques.

# Christmas Stocking Garland

Create a festive look in your home with this delightful Christmas garland made up of 15 tiny socks hanging on a wide red gingham ribbon. You could turn this into an advent calendar: just make ten more and embroider a number on the front of each.

**Measurements**
Each sock is 9 cm (3½ in) high

**Materials**
2 x 50 g (2 oz) balls Heirloom Merino 4-ply baby wool, red
1 x 50 g (2 oz) ball of white faux fur wool
4 x 2.25 mm (US 1) double-pointed knitting needles
2 m (78 in) x 4 cm (1¾ in) wide red gingham ribbon

15 red buttons 1 cm (⅜ in) diameter
Wool needle
Red sewing thread
Sewing needle

# SOCKS
## Make 15

Using 3 x 2.25 mm knitting needles and white yarn, cast on 24 sts (8, 8, 8).

Knit 2 rounds.

Break of white yarn and join in red.

**Round 1**: Knit, inc 2 sts evenly on each needle (30 sts).

Work 20 rounds st st (every round knit).

## DIVIDE FOR HEEL

**Next round**: K7, sl last 7 sts from needle three onto same needle (14 heel sts – these will be worked backwards and forwards in rows)

Divide rem sts between 2 needles

**Row 1**: Sl 1, purl to end.

**Row 2**: *Sl 1, K1, rep from * to last st, K1.

Rep these 2 rows another 4 times and then row 1 once.

### TURN HEEL

K9, turn, P4, turn, K3, k2tog, K1, turn, P4, p2tog, P1, turn, K5, k2tog, K1, turn, cont in this manner until all sts have been worked onto one needle (8 sts). Knit back 4 sts.

Place instep sts back on one needle.

Commencing at centre heel, K4, pick up and K9 sts along side of heel. With next needle knit across instep sts; with next needle pick up and K9 sts along other side of heel, knit rem 4 heel sts. Knitting is now back in the round.

Decrease for Instep

**Round 1**: Knit

**Round 2**: First needle, K to last 3 sts, k2tog, K1; second needle, knit; third needle, sl 1, K1, psso, knit to end.

Rep these two rounds until there are 8 sts left on needle one and three and 16 sts on needle two.

DECREASE FOR TOE

**Round 1**: Knit.

**Round 2**: First needle, K to last 3 sts, k2tog, K1; second needle, sl 1, K1, psso, knit to last 3 sts, k2tog, K1; third needle, sl 1, K1, psso, knit to end.

Rep these two rounds until 4 sts rem on needle one and three, and 8 sts rem on needle two. Divide sts evenly on to two needles.

Graft toe sts together (see techniques).

Darn in loose ends.

## To Make Up

Turn in double hem at each end of the ribbon, and then a 6 cm (2¼ in) loop for hanging. Stitch in place.

Arrange the socks evenly along the length of ribbon with half the toes pointing in one direction and the other half in the other direction. Using red thread stitch through the back of the sock and ribbon, then take up a button. The tops of the stockings should be 1 cm (³/₈ in) above the top of the ribbon. Stitch in place.

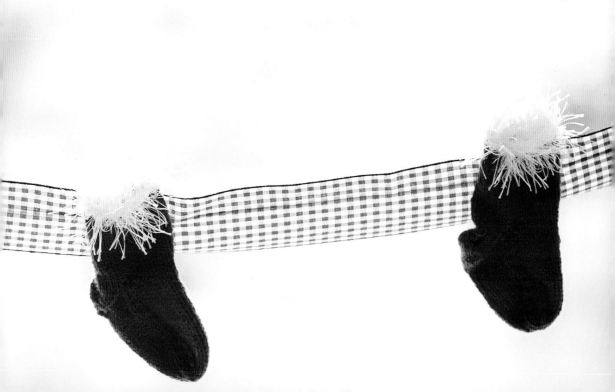

# Templates

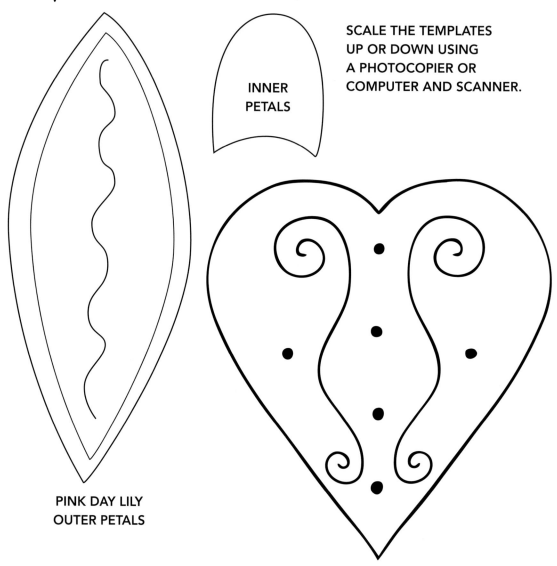

INNER
PETALS

SCALE THE TEMPLATES
UP OR DOWN USING
A PHOTOCOPIER OR
COMPUTER AND SCANNER.

PINK DAY LILY
OUTER PETALS

LAVENDER HEART.
USE OUTLINE FOR APPLIQUÉ COT BLANKET AND
CROCHETED HEART MOTIF FOR VEST

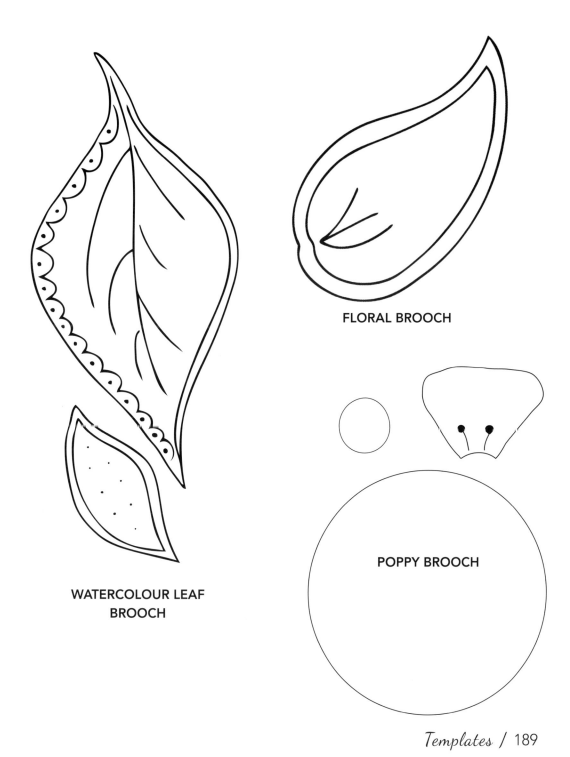

FLORAL BROOCH

WATERCOLOUR LEAF
BROOCH

POPPY BROOCH

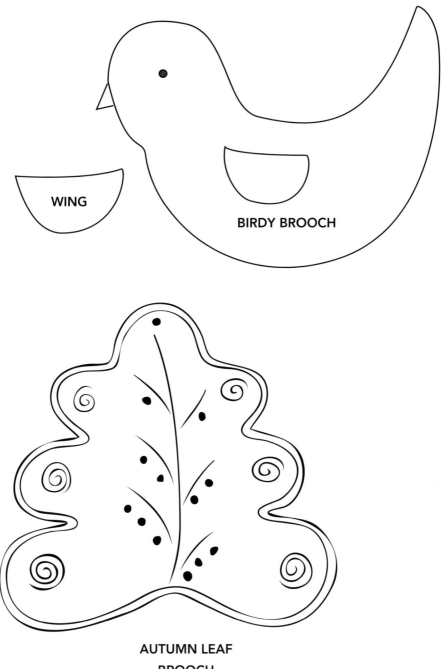

WING

BIRDY BROOCH

AUTUMN LEAF
BROOCH

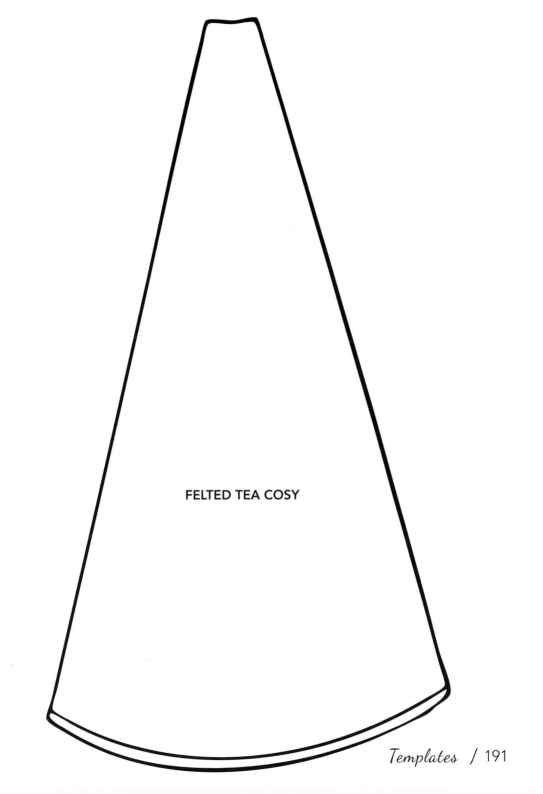

FELTED TEA COSY

# Index

# Acknowledgements

My mother taught me to embroider when I was very young and it must have been a trying business for her.
I am left-handed and I am sure was particularly bad tempered.
This book is for my beautiful daughter Felicity who has always gratefully received all manner of weird gifts,
way before I really got the hang of the whole knitting and sewing business
I would like to thank Lliane Clarke for encouraging me to write my
third book and having faith in me.
Please contact me via my website www.dropstitchdesign.com if you are unsure about any of
the instructions in this book.